Nobody's Little Girl Anymore

Nobody's Little Girl Anymore

Cynthia Beardslee

ISBN: 978-1-944662-68-4

Publishing date: September 2021

Cover Illustration by Carleigh Beardslee & Jacqueline Kahler

Dedication

This book is dedicated to my dad, of course!.

Contents

Dedication v

Chapter 1: Dad 1

Chapter 2: Memories 13

Chapter 3: Lessons Learned 25

Chapter 4: That Reminds Me… 45

Chapter 5: Young James Dean 53

Chapter 6: One Day at a Time 61

Chapter 7: Time for Mourning 91

Chapter 8: New Beginnings 111

Chapter 9: Mirror Image 127

Chapter 10: Old Wounds 131

Epilogue 135

Author Bio 139

Chapter 1: Dad

As a little girl, if I allowed the thought of my dad not being here someday to enter my mind and dig itself deeper into my thoughts, the darkest of fears and sadness would overwhelm and cripple me. This sadness would be so intense and all-consuming that my throat would tighten, and my eyes would well and overflow with tears that immediately streamed down my cheeks. A sudden, overpowering wave of sorrow and dread would wash over me, literally taking my breath away.

I think most of us have that one person who holds the deepest and most loving, intense memories for us. You know what I'm talking about. Those times when you recall the past and there is that one person who is the main character in those memories that you hold so close and cherish. These memories can make you laugh, cry, recall nostalgic days of yesteryear; they may even stir up feelings of anger, disappointment, or sadness. That one person that changed you in some way, big or small, whether they realized it or not. That person made such an impact that your love, appreciation, respect, admiration, friendship, kinship for him or her touched your soul deeply. The absence of this special person is a hurt so extreme that you can't truly explain it until it happens. Their absence becomes a black hole in your life, one that could never be filled by anyone else or totally healed. Your life is changed...forever. For me, that one person was my dad.

I have always been a daddy's girl. Even as my fiftieth birthday approached, I realized I needed my dad as much as I did when I was a little girl.

* * *

March 26, 2018: As I sit in my dad's living room, I hear a humming noise coming from the back room, his computer room as he calls it. He is using the nebulizer to help him with his breathing. Over the past two weeks, we have spent every moment of every day together. There has not been one stone left unturned, no word left unsaid. We have laughed, cried, sat silently lost in thought, and have shared many words of love and gratitude for each other. Over these two weeks, I have watched my dad's health change and not for the better. Only six days ago, we found out my dad has terminal lung cancer that has metastasized to other areas in his 80-year-old body. He has decided to forego any biopsy, oncology consult, and treatment. In his words, "Why do I need someone from the outside to tell me what I already know is going on, on the inside?"

The man that I have called Dad for almost 50 years is a gift. He is the greatest dad ever. With that said, I realize he isn't perfect, and he never tries to be. He has his faults just like the rest of us. My dad has a hot temper. Growing up, what Richard said was *law*. I never once dared to challenge his rules of the house. Even those times when he got mad, he spoke with a firm, stern voice, he would discipline me, and then it was over. My dad never carried around anger or a grudge. But when he got mad, he laid down the law. My dad either liked you or he didn't. No matter how true a friend he had been to someone, if they misused his trust or friendship, he was done with them.

My dad was a sarcastic, tell-it-like-it-is, no nonsense kind of man. He never was touchy-feely but occasionally pulled me close, hugged me tight, and told me he loved me. Never overly emotional about things, he would sit and talk in his deep voice that also had a comforting softness about it. He let me know when I'd done wrong, but he also spoke those words with a tone of love and learning and often said, "Mistakes aren't bad; it's when we refuse to learn from them that they become destructive."

Even in his disciplining, he always showed love and allowed me to reflect and learn from his words and/or actions. As his little girl, the times when I struggled, made a mistake, or was upset for any reason, my dad had this way of relating to me. Kneeling down so he could get close to me and speak eye-to-eye, his voice would grow soft, his strong yet at the same time gentle arm would quietly and lovingly slip around my shoulders, and he would say, "Listen; think about it. What did we just talk about? What would you do differently?" He always had this way of making me think things through.

My dad has always been my biggest fan, always encouraging, praising, and showing his support no matter what. In his own mind, he was a realist, yet he always told me I could do anything I put my mind to if I was willing to put in the hard work and to expect the unexpected.

In my early days as a tiny, blue-eyed, blonde tomboy growing up in the northwestern mountains of Sussex County, New Jersey, he was to me a Charles Ingalls kind of dad—constantly patient and taking the time to teach me all about nature, how to treat creatures, big and small, of all kinds, with kindness and respect. He spoke *to* me, not *at* me, and everything we did together had a lesson. They were mostly fun adventures, and, yes, I remember all of those lessons and have hopefully passed some of them on to my children. He taught me that it was okay to go outside, play in the dirt, and get really dirty, climb trees, and explore the mountains, streams, and nature that surrounded our house.

The man I remember from my childhood is a casual, no-nonsense man. He had black hair in his younger days, and it was always thin. He always wore his hair is a kind of Elvis swoop in the front. He never had a mustache or beard. He had these beautiful, deep dimples. Even as an adult, he had this devilish look to his smile. With a sly gaze in his eyes, always with an expression like he was up to no good, that smile would appear. You would wonder what he was thinking. That smile showed off this big separation between his two front teeth. He told the story more than once that he still had a few baby teeth when he enlisted in the Marines. During his physical, they sat him down, grabbed some medical apparatus that had the appearance of a wrench, and yanked out those teeth!

My dad rarely dressed up, truly almost never. In my younger days, he always wore worn, faded jeans and a short-sleeve T-shirt. During the summer, his favorite outfit was shorts and a T-shirt and in winter it was a flannel shirt and jeans. Mind you, most of his clothing was stained with some kind of paint, oil, or concoction from working in the garage. Fifty years later, his fashion sense (or lack thereof) hadn't changed.

I guess I was about three or so when my first memory of my dad imprinted on my young mind. We lived in a tiny, two-story Cape Cod style house in Livingston, New Jersey. It had a modest yard with a fenced backyard. My first memory of my dad remains vivid to this day. It was wintertime, and, as he often did, my dad put his wool coat on, slid his feet into his clunky, black, plastic, winter boots, and made his way out the back door that was off our kitchen. This door led to a few stairs that took you to our backyard. Once outside, he'd make his way through the snow, leaving patterned footprints as he trekked his way to the fence that lined the edge of our yard. Each breath made a small white puff that lifted and slowly disappeared above him. Walking along the length of the fence, he left a peanut, still in its shell, about every six inches. I intently watched him through the back door window, waiting for him to come inside. When he returned to the house, he shook off the bitter cold of a New Jersey winter. He scooped me up in his arms and stood in front of the kitchen sink, where we had full visibility of the backyard through the window. He perched my tiny bottom on the edge of the sink, and I leaned back into his arms that protectively wrapped themselves around me. I sat and we waited for what in my three-year-old mind seemed like hours. Within minutes, we saw them: curious, fuzzy, grey-brown squirrels with fluffy tails. Just a few minutes earlier, I imagine they cautiously watched my father place the peanuts along the fence. These squirrels made their way down from the snow-covered trees, checking out those oddly-shaped little goodies on the fence. As we watched, I could feel the warmth of my dad's arms around my tiny body. As his cheek drew closer to mine, I could smell the hint of coffee on his breath, feel the chill from the outside on his skin, and touch the roughness of his five o'clock shadow as it tickled my cheek.

He pointed and whispered, "Look, do you see them?"

I followed his finger, and there they were, predictable and hungry. We spotted the first squirrel making its way down the tree, taking a long leap from the tree trunk to the fence, hopping along the top of the fence to where the first peanut was placed. So began the arduous task of collecting as many peanuts as possible before the other squirrels descended on these treasures. The entertaining part was when a squirrel would work relentlessly trying to figure out how to fit all those peanuts in its mouth. Putting one in, jamming another one in, only to take both out, try a different one, then another, rearranging them each time with the hopes that all the peanuts would fit. Those tiny paws, resembling hands, holding each peanut, turning and rearranging it just so. The end result was one per customer. My dad would smile and so would I, mostly reacting to his enjoyment of this little movie that played out before us on a cold, snowy, New Jersey afternoon.

Why is this memory not only the first but probably the one that had the biggest impact on my life and helped shape me into the person I am today? It's because in that simple, peaceful, bonding moment, my dad showed his true colors as a father, a person, and a man. He instilled in me several values by that one act. He taught me to appreciate the little things and that we have a choice to find enjoyment in everything. We should never be too busy to stop and live in the moment. He continued to show me the same values over and over through almost everything he did. He was always taking care of, tending to, and helping animals just as he did that day. And I knew he would be that way till the day he took his last breath. With that one act, he infused me with a passion and love for animals that I have passed on to my children. All life matters—all life.

Fast forward to today, April 1, 2018, Easter Sunday. Today is a good day. The sun is shining, the Carolina blue sky is the bluest we've seen in a while. The temperature is a warm 71 degrees. The pollen is almost in full bloom, which is evident by the pale-yellow dust on everyone's cars. My sinuses and my dull headache also remind me that the pollen is performing its yearly ritual. Nature is waking up, birds are chirping, cardinals seem to be everywhere, finding their mates. The wind chimes on my dad's porch are serenading us while we take in the day. Bees are hard at work and making their way from flower to flower. I can hear little voices of children playing and dogs barking in the distance. Life is good. God is good. My dad is here; he is feeling better today.

Yesterday and last night were a little rough. He was shaky, trembling from the Prednisone he is taking for his breathing, and he's decided, "Enough—no more Prednisone."

He has tenderness in his upper left lung area. He hasn't been sleeping all that well. But, today, we shared our cup of morning coffee on the front porch together. His dog, Goober, enjoyed sunning himself while Dad and I simply took in each other's company and the beautiful day before us without small talk. In a little while, my son, Bryce, will be here to help his Papa clean up the garage and take down shelves. Then my dad, Bryce, my daughter, Carleigh, and I will enjoy Easter dinner prepared by the master chef himself, Dad, aka Papa.

I reflect and realize that this is the last Easter I will celebrate with my dad. April 9th will also be my dad's eightieth birthday, his last birthday. This realization is bittersweet as I am thankful for this day and also saddened by the harsh reality that the man I have known for 50 years, who has been my biggest supporter, friend, and mentor will at some point in the near future no longer be just a phone call or a five-minute drive away.

Saturday, March 17, started off like any other day. My dad and I spent the afternoon together, meandering through mobile homes (something he liked to do). I dropped him off that afternoon, went home and spent the evening cooking dinner and hanging out with my kids.

Carleigh and I were just leaving church that brisk, early spring Sunday morning when I checked my phone and saw that my dad had left me a voicemail.

"Cyn (one of several nicknames he had for me), uh, we have a problem. Can you come over when you can?"

We made our way to my dad's house, and Carleigh dropped me off and went on to do the food shopping for me.

I walked in my dad's house and he was sitting in his favorite chair, wearing the same sweater he always wore. Goober, his adorable, faithful, canine sidekick was curled up next to him.

"What's going on, Dad?" When I had listened to his message, I could clearly tell in his voice he was concerned. Now seeing his face, that was visible.

He bluntly said, "I lost the use of my legs last night."

"What?" I said, confused. This made no sense to me; we had just spent the entire afternoon walking through at least a dozen modular homes, and he was fine just 24 hours earlier.

He went on to explain that the previous night, as he let Goober outside, he bent down to pick up his leash and lost the ability to stand up and fell right down. Thankfully, his friend Billy was there and helped my dad back into the house. He shared that he was extremely weak and did not feel comfortable walking.

Worry set in. But my father also taught me that life turns on a dime, and you have to go with those changes.

I began staying with my dad as of that day. I spent the nights at his house and worked half days at the office. Then I spent a few hours at home with my kids, packed up work clothes for the next day, and headed back to my dad's.

This has been my life for three weeks, and in that time my life has altered more than I could ever imagine.

Within these three emotional, overwhelming, fear-filled, long yet gone in the blink of an eye weeks, so much has changed. Prior to Sunday, March 18, I had so much of my life planned out, or so I thought, and my dad was a big part of that plan.

In August, I will be an empty nester. My youngest, Carleigh, will be heading off to college out of state. My oldest, Bryce, has been living at home but has potential plans to move out sometime in the near future. Three years ago, I met the love of my life. He just happens to live on a beautiful, 36-foot Catalina sailboat on the North Carolina Coast in the small historic town of New Bern, which is two and a half hours from where I currently live. My dad has always loved the water and the beach, so the logical thing to do would be to sell my house, which would be too big without the children, and relocate to where my boyfriend lives and bring my dad with me. This made total sense, and everyone was on board with the idea.

I am an only child; my mom passed away 12 years ago, and my dad and I, well, we were all we had besides my children and my cousin Claudia, who lived halfway across the country. My boyfriend welcomed and was excited about our plans. So, over the last few months, we had been looking at property and places to live in and around New Bern. I was in the process of polishing up my resume, and my dad even started going through his house, cleaning and throwing things out, and he began the arduous task of packing.

My dad was beyond happy and said, "Nothing could be better than the thought of spending the rest of my days by the water, fishing and crabbing whenever I can, and just enjoying life."

With tear-filled eyes, I realized this would never be. As I wrote these words, I sat on my dad's couch. Glancing to my left, I noticed a box with the words "living room" written in thick black marker in my dad's writing, testament to the dream of moving to the coast. Straight ahead of me, the oxygen tank my dad now needed to help with his breathing sat idly waiting its next usage. So much had changed. How? Why? If I dwelled on it too long, I knew I would break down, and now was not the time for falling apart. This was the time to cherish the moments I still had with him. I would have years ahead to mourn for him.

But for now, I fought back the tears and smiled. *Today, at this moment, life is good*, I thought.

That first week, the week of March 18, remains somewhat of a blur. I, we, were definitely in survival mode. That first week my dad went for X-rays, blood tests, scans, and an MRI. He kept telling me that "this wasn't going to be good." I kept praying and reached out to my closest and dearest asking for prayers. I had to remain positive until we knew for sure what we were dealing with.

Dr. Gowala, my dad's family doctor, called the following Monday and asked that we come in for the results. I was sick to my stomach as I thought to myself, "If the results were good, he would've just told dad over the phone." I did a lot of praying up until that doctor's appointment.

We arrived at Dr. Gowala's office around 3:20 for our 3:30 appointment. His office was about a mile from my dad's house. Prior to the doctor's appointment, we were both silent, lost in thought and worry. All I could do was pray. I knew this was out of my hands, but with my faith I would be able to deal with whatever lay ahead of us.

As Dr. Gowala led us back to the examination room, every step I took, every sound, smell, thought seemed to happen in slow motion. My senses were heightened. I heard every noise. Every color around me was bright and vibrant. That walk down the brightly painted purple hallway took a mere few seconds but felt like an eternity.

"You have lung cancer that has metastasized to the bones and the nodes on your liver."

Those words, those damn words, I will remember with such clarity, sadness, and fear for the rest of my days. Those words took my breath away. Because I sat to the right of my dad with Dr.

Gowala positioned off to our left, my dad couldn't see the tears streaming down my cheeks. Dr. Gowala looked past my dad and made eye contact with me. The look on his face softened. He gave me a gentle nod, acknowledging my tears.

Glancing at my father, I reached for his arm and held on tight. A man who has never shown much emotion, especially sadness or fear, my dad couldn't contain his feelings completely at that moment. Looking at his profile, I could see his chin quiver and his eyes well with tears.

"Hell, I don't have a snowball's chance in hell," my father said, an ever so spot-on response.

Dr. Gowala apologized to us for having to deliver such sad news.

For years, my father had repeated that if he ever got the news of a terminal diagnosis, he would forego the tests and treatments. Apparently, based on the shortness of this office visit and no suggestion of a biopsy or treatment, he had made his wishes known to Dr. Gowala.

He shook my father's hand and said, "If you need anything, please let me know."

"Thanks, Doc" was all my dad said in his soft, saddened voice.

The two-minute drive back to my dad's house was quiet. My mind boiled like a volcano about to erupt, exploding with a million emotions and thoughts. What can I say about those next few hours? We were both lost in thought, absorbing the realization of what we were just told. We were trying to take it all in. So many questions, so many fears, what ifs, if onlys, and what nows?

Back home, my dad lit a cigarette and stood on the porch in silence. His lip quivered and his hand shook as he drew the cigarette close to his lips. He took one drag after another. There was nothing to say. I called my cousin Claudia, my dad's niece; they had always been close. We lost my Aunt Marie, Claudia's mom and my dad's sister, 12 years earlier to the same horrendous disease. As soon as I heard Claudia's voice, I broke down. I lost it and began to uncontrollably sob. The only thought going through my mind was, "How can I watch the strongest person I know slowly suffer and die?"

Crying, I told Claudia the news. She reassured me that we would get through this, we would help my dad, keep him comfortable. She reminded me that Grandma, Grandpa, Uncle Jimmy, Aunt Marie, and Mom were all there on the other side, waiting for him.

"When it's his time, they will be there to help him cross over," she said.

Chapter 2: Memories

My dad gave me the best childhood ever! Of the countless memories etched on my mind, most were wonderful, some were sad, but I came away learning so much from them all.

Anyone reading this who is a "Daddy's Girl" will be able to relate. However, if you were lucky enough to truly be close to a parent, you, we, were blessed.

The nicknames…he had a few for me: Cyn, kiddo, little one, and, my favorite, Squirt. Most of us can relate to the nicknames we were given in our younger days—some cute, some funny, and some we would rather forget. Maybe we can agree, however, that as we grew older and wiser, those nicknames evoked fond memories of days gone by. That was certainly true for me.

In the last chapter, I shared in my first memory of my father. Since then, there have been countless more sprinkled throughout our 50 years as father and daughter.

Throughout my life, my dad was well known for repeating several one-liners with a mixture of sarcasm and humor but always with truth. Most were the kind everyone has heard before, but he reiterated them endlessly.

"You can bring a horse to water…"

"Don't put the cart before the horse."

"Don't worry about things you can't change."

"This too shall pass."

"What doesn't kill us makes us stronger."

"Life is what you make it."

"I have patience with children because they don't know any better. I don't have patience with adults because they should…"

"Life is too short to worry about impressing others."

"Anything worth doing is worth doing right."

"Be flattered when others talk about you. They have nothing better to do with their time than think and talk about you."

I could go on and on. Some of his more flamboyant one-liners were meant for the situation at that time, and colorful and blunt they were! One of my favorite expressions he said often was "Just for shit and giggles." When referring to the power of an engine in a vehicle, he would say, "It has some shit and git." I've repeated this one frequently through the years and just the other day heard my son use this for the first time.

I was one lucky girl growing up. All the kids on the block (especially the boys) wanted to hang out with my dad. He had an uncanny amount of patience when it came to kids of all ages. When interacting with children, my dad would get on their level, soften his voice, and *show* them what he was talking about. He went into great detail, explaining things to them, and he even shared a story based on his experience. He took the time to listen as well. He would ask them a question to make them think about what they saw, felt, and heard. He was always calm and loved to see a child's reaction to what they were hearing. He never dismissed a child—never—in that moment when they were learning, soaking it all in. In those hundreds of times with my dad, I learned so much and I remember it all. I'm not sure where he got that ability. He said his mom had the patience of a saint when he was younger, so maybe it came from her.

I remember my grandma well. She was a kind, gentle, intelligent woman. I don't have any memories of her raising her voice or being angry. She was usually quiet but never one to be underestimated. Being widowed by the time she was in her 40s, in the late 1940s, she was self-reliant and resilient. She worked full-time and supported her family, which was not typical in that day and time. According to other family members, raising my dad was no small undertaking. He was, as I understand it, an absolute hellion. My grandfather passed away when my dad was about nine, so I never had the chance to meet the man who had a hand in molding my father, but I am grateful nonetheless. Whoever or whatever circumstances molded my dad to be the man he became, I am grateful and blessed beyond words.

On more than one occasion, one of the boys who lived in our neighborhood would make their way up our front lawn to our sidewalk that led to our front door. Being a teenage girl, I was shy but anxiously anticipated that they might, hopefully, be coming to the door to talk to me. No such luck.

"Hi, is your dad home?"

Really? I was disappointed on several occasions! These boys would ask my dad to take them fishing. They all had fathers but came to hang out with *my* dad. He was always willing to take them fishing, hiking, or camping in the mountains behind my house. My dad only had one law: "My house, my rules. Respect me, and I'll respect you." Every single one of those boys respected him and they got along famously.

My dad always taught me to respect myself as well.

"Respect yourself; never lower your standards. Those that matter in your life will respect you too."

Well said, Dad, well said. This statement has served me throughout my life.

My dad's sense of humor was always tongue in cheek and sarcastic, and he loved to play practical jokes. Two instances that stand out in my mind. My oldest and one of my dearest friends, Tammy, lived across the street one house to the right of us. We've known each other for over 45 years. Tammy was, well, the only way to put it is that she was a "pain in the ass" as a friend. Out of my small circle of besties, she was the bossy one, the one that had to control everything; everything had to go her way. Tammy decided what we played, who would be partners with whom, who was her best friend (this changed frequently), and who we could and couldn't talk to. A little tidbit about Tammy: She was deathly afraid of the dark. On hot summer nights, if we happened to be at a friend's down the street, walking home we *had* to walk past our own homes and accompany her to her house. She instructed us to watch her from the street as she made her way through her yard and safely to her front door. We weren't allowed to leave until she securely closed her front door behind her. If she was on her way to one of our houses after dark, we had to make sure the front light was on and had to watch her cross the street, waiting for her arrival.

When I was growing up, our front yard sloped upwards slightly towards our house. A group of three or four trees stood in the middle of the yard next to the sidewalk from the driveway. Off to the right, about a quarter way from the street, there was another cluster of trees just about on the property line between our yard and our neighbor's. Like any other night that Tammy was on her way over, I had to stand guard at the entry door with the front light on while I watched her cautiously make her way out her front door. She'd walk anxiously at a steady clip to the top of her driveway, then hurriedly sprint across the street, up my yard and to my front door, avoiding the grips of whatever could be lurking in the shadows.

One particular night, my dad decided to have a little fun with Tammy. He hid behind the group of trees to the right of our house. Blending perfectly with the outline of the trees, he patiently waited for Tammy's approach. As predictable as ever, Tammy anxiously and with quick steps made her way across the street. I could see her long, dark, chocolate brown hair bouncing as she ran. She was dressed in a white T-shirt, Jordache jeans, and cool white Nike sneakers with a simple, single red swoosh that were at the time all the rage. As soon as she approached the group of the trees where my dad was hiding, he jumped out, hunched over like the hunchback of Notre Dame. Swinging the arm that hung lower, dragging the opposite leg, he was moaning a sickly, eerie wail. Without glancing to see what or who it could be, Tammy let out this scream from the top of her lungs, a high-pitched teenage girl screech. Her shriek of terror was ear-piercing. She frantically ran all the way to my front door and quickly looped around the cluster of trees in the middle of our yard. She continued screaming and flailing her arms as she rounded those trees and ran down our yard, across the street, and into her house, slamming the door behind her.

To a person reading this who did not have the pleasure of knowing Tammy personally, this might seem like a cruel joke. But to those of us who did and do know her and her incessant nagging about doing things her way, this was freaking hysterical, and, yes, a bit of payback.

One other time that I fondly remember my dad having some fun was on a particular camping trip we took with Tammy's family. Her family had a modest-sized camper while we camped in a 10-man tent. Yes, the three of us in a 10-man tent. My mom's goal was to make it as homey as possible. We slept on lawn chairs and had various, multi-colored and mis-matched remnants of carpet that my mom brought along so we had something soft to walk on, not just the cold, hard ground. Our other bits of home included a large lantern that lit up the entire tent, a broom to keep the floor clean, and a full-length mirror. Yes, a mirror. For what? Maybe to check on how we looked after a few days without showering.

Each night, we built a campfire and all of us gathered around it roasting marshmallows and talking. If memory serves me, my dad, my mom, Tammy, her parents, Billy, her younger brother, and I had crowded around the fire that night. On this night around the campfire, we happened to be talking about Bigfoot and bears.

Somehow—and I can't recall exactly how—Tammy, my dad, and I were able to get away from the gathering. There was a large, open field behind our campsite. At some point, I guess we thought it would be a good idea to wander through that open field and scare the crap out of the others. Tammy, Dad, and I stealthily crept through the field. We could easily see everyone sitting around the fire. As we got closer to the campsite, my dad tossed a rock that would land somewhere off in the distance but close enough for them to hear. After a few tosses, Tammy's younger brother heard the rocks.

Looking somewhat surprised and curious, Billy asked, "Did you hear that?" He was now alert, glancing around to see what could possibly be making the sounds.

An old, barbed wire fence with wooden posts ran along the open field. The grass along the fence was high—around two to three feet or so. Tammy, Dad, and I crouched behind that grass. My dad gently pulled on the fence, and it made a slight rustling sound against the grass. After a few times of tugging on the fence, Tammy's dad and Billy became more than curious and wanted to investigate what was behind these noises. We were fighting back the giggles as Tammy's dad stood up, trying to look tough, as he and Billy looking around warily.

"Did you hear that!?" Billy said, his voice heightened and scared.

Tammy's dad went to their camper, returning with a flashlight. Concerned and curious, Billy asked, "What could it be, Dad?"

Tammy's dad shook his head, "Not sure. A bear?"

My mom and Tammy's mom stayed behind as Billy and his dad cautiously took a few steps closer to the fence. My dad gently shook the fence again, causing the rustling sound against the grass. Tammy's dad and Billy froze where they were standing. We watched as Billy tightly grabbed his dad's arm, taking a step behind him.

"Dad, I think it's a bear. What should we do?"

Holding back our desire to burst out laughing, we sat, watched, and waited. When they took a few more cautious steps forward, my dad gave a small nod and we jumped up, springing to our feet, roaring and growling as loudly as we could. At that moment, all we saw was the bright, circular light from the flashlight that Tammy's dad was holding jump from his hands as it made a flashing, crazy zig-zag pattern in the dark of the night. Both of them shrieked, abandoning their bravery and the flashlight as they ran back to the campsite as fast as their feet would take them.

Besides being a jokester and a wiseass, my dad was always one of the smartest people I ever knew. For those familiar with the show *Cheers*, he was quite the Cliff Clavin of information. He was always full of knowledge as he shared experiences and tidbits of wisdom throughout my childhood. My dad was not a "book smart" kind of man. He never liked school, studying, or tests, and dropped out at the age of sixteen. He eventually went back and got his GED. However, he had a lifetime full of knowledge. His smarts came from living life, making mistakes, learning, and growing from them.

He said this himself: "I don't know a lot about one particular thing. But I know a little about almost everything."

If you asked him about something, he'd be able to provide facts, the *how-to*, and would give great detail about whatever you asked. But, if you asked him about something he didn't know, he would tell you so. He was never one to pretend to understand something to impress people or make small talk.

Growing up in the northwestern region of New Jersey, we were surrounded by mountains and rolling hills. I fondly remember walking through the mountains that were behind the house where I grew up. We'd walk along the railroad tracks, not saying much, just enjoying the day and nature. If we stumbled upon a rock formation, a bug, a tree, a flower, he would walk me to it, we'd observe, and maybe touch it. No matter what it was, he would be able to provide a little knowledge about it. I learned so much about many, many things from him.

As I think back now about those times growing up with the man I was lucky enough to call my dad, I am humbled. I realize now I took all of it for granted at the time, because spending my childhood with a dad who was involved, patient, and hands-on, was the norm for me. I hate to admit it now, but a lot of the times where he made me stay with him and do things—whether it was yardwork, planting the garden in the spring, digging for worms for fishing, fixing the car, or running to the local Rockaway Sales aka Sussex County's version of True Value—those were the times and memories that I most fondly look back on and wish to God I could go back to. Hindsight!

When we first moved into our house, the backyard was a mess. It was nothing but overgrown weeds at least three feet high. Trying to make it easier to mow, my dad took a machete to it. Unfortunately, he came upon a rabbit's den without knowing it, and for the mom, it was too late. My dad felt horrible. Reaching into the den, he pulled out six or so of the tiniest little bunnies. They were only a few days old, eyes still closed, fur not fully covering their bodies. They were so small and delicate. He carefully wrapped them in a blanket and brought them inside. He cleaned out a big fish tank we had and filled it with cedar clippings and torn newspaper. One by one, he gently placed those sweet little babies in the tank, positioning a heat lamp above them to keep them warm. With each step, he would narrate what he was doing so I would understand. With an eye dropper, he mashed up some food and liquid (I do not recall what this concoction was), and we fed them a few times a day. He was diligent about keeping them warm and fed; he wanted so badly to save those babies. Unfortunately, none of them survived. It was such an unselfish act of kindness and love. I loved my dad for that sweet attempt to save them.

Every year we planted a garden. My dad loved gardening and had a green thumb. When he took the time, he could make our yard look beautiful. Honestly, however, he was not fond of the pruning and weed pulling. His favorite flowers were tulips and azaleas. Each spring, like clockwork, we would turn over that little patch of land in our backyard, adding manure and lime and raking it. Then the arduous task of planting began. By the time I was eight or so, I knew the process well. Every two inches, I would poke my tiny index finger into the ground, and he'd follow behind me, dropping a few of the seeds in each hole. We would start from the beginning, cover each hole with fresh soil, making sure to water it well. We grew everything: corn, tomatoes, zucchini, green beans, squash, carrots, lettuce. We weeded, we watered, we picked, we cooked, and we ate!

Alongside that garden there was a small rock wall that consisted of a single row of large rocks; it was no more than 8 to 10 inches high—just enough to border the garden. That rock wall holds some special memories for me. Not only do I think of all the years of planting a garden with my dad, but I also smile when I recall the many times we spent watching chipmunks run, jump, and scoot across the wall as well.

Flash back to my opening memory of my dad with the squirrels and the peanuts along the fence. The chipmunks provided similar entertainment during summer months. At the corner of the rock wall around our garden, there was a large stone, which was around two feet wide by two feet high. On hot summer days, we placed a few peanuts (unshelled) on the rock and sat at our picnic table, watching and waiting. Before long, the curiosity of those adorable, playful chipmunks got the best of them, and they made their way to that big corner rock to check out what was waiting for them. They'd come from the woods and hop along the rock wall. Like the squirrels in winter, these little critters tirelessly worked at fitting more than one peanut in their tiny mouths. Eventually giving in to only taking one peanut, they would run off with their small treasure, tail straight in the air like a flagpole.

Another moment spent enjoying and appreciating the little things. Forty-some years later, that memory remains vivid in my mind and heart. My dad loved all creatures, big and small, and passed down that same love to me. Thank you, Dad.

I started fishing with my dad around the age of three or four. It was a pastime he loved. I believe trout fishing was his favorite because that was what we did most. In New Jersey, trout season opened the first weekend in April. The night before, after dark, my dad and I would venture out to our backyard, flashlight and bucket in hand. Carefully walking through the damp, green blades of grass in the backyard, we aimed our flashlights at the ground, and there they would be: night crawlers. Long, slippery suckers, we'd have to be quick to grab them; they would stretch and, if we weren't careful, we would miss them. Our grip had to be just *so*—tight enough to not let them literally slip through our fingers but not so strong they would break—gross. Into the bucket with dirt, they would go, bait for our fishing trip the next morning.

At the break of dawn on the first Saturday in April, we'd wake up, eat breakfast, which consisted of my dad's light, fluffy, and sweet homemade pancakes and bacon. My dad would load a thermos of coffee, fishing rods, tackle, and our bait consisting of the previous night's catch of night crawlers into the car along with a cooler for the day's catch, and we'd make our way to the brook down the hill. The air had an early spring chill to it; the ground around the stream was damp, squishy. The birds were chirping as the sun rose, warming the air. The trees were just starting to bud their first leaves for the season.

I have a confession: I don't love fishing. Oh, when we're actually catching fish, it's lots of fun. But, if we're having an off day, cast after cast and not even a nibble, fishing is the last thing I want to do. However, my father could fish all day without a catch or even a nibble....Yawn. In my younger days, I thought the mention of having to go to the bathroom would be my way out. Nope, without breaking his concentration, without even taking his eyes off the tip of his rod, cigarette hanging out of the corner of his mouth, my dad would point to a bush off in the distance, and that was my bathroom for the day.

My dad never kept fish that were small. He always released them to give them a chance to grow and have offspring of their own. He knew the importance of keeping only what we were going to eat, allowing Mother Nature to do her job and make sure there was always enough fish for later fishing trips. At the end of the day, we'd bring home our "keepers," and I had the job of cleaning them. He taught me early how to properly clean fish. As my dad would say, "You catch them, you clean them." Once they were all cleaned, my dad would bread and fry them. He made the best fried fish ever! He'd make his fabulous potato salad, and we'd feast!

He was also a fabulous cook. My mom didn't really like to cook, but she was one heck of a housekeeper. Our house was always tidy, I slept in clean sheets, wore clean clothes, ate off of clean plates. Floors were spotless. Cooking was simply not her forte. My grandmother, my dad's mom, was also a really good cook. My dad was raised in a household where eating large, old-fashioned, meat and potato meals was the norm. When my dad cooked, it was always a tender roast with vegetables or stews, soups, or Danish or Hungarian dishes from his heritage. Without fail, he always served bread or hot rolls with these meals. The house was always filled with the aroma of spices, tender beef simmering, and hot bread. He enjoyed eating and cooking equally. Some of my favorite dishes of his, and there were many, were beef stroganoff, fried fish, fried zucchini, paella, sour cream chicken, his homemade shrimp salad, potato salad, homemade cheesecake, and Danish Christmas cookies. Just to name a few.

Chapter 3: Lessons Learned

My dad always was my biggest fan and supported and loved me through every decision I ever made—whether or not he felt it was the right thing to do at the time. Once I was an adult and on my own, he continued to show his love and support.

During my childhood, he was my father, disciplinarian, and teacher. As an adult, my dad became my best friend. During some tough times in my life as an adult, in my marriage, or raising my kids as a single parent, he was always there for me. Sometimes he would just listen and say, "Cyn, I don't know what to tell you. I wish I could help you. All I can say is this will pass. It will all work out. Trust me." I always felt a sense of calm when he told me this. His words never failed to bring me peace.

As I'm writing this, I realize a similarity in the relationship between my dad and me and mine with my son. During my son's childhood, I was his parent, disciplinarian, and hopefully teacher. As a single parent, there were several occasions when my son tried me. But now that he is an adult, our relationship is slowly transitioning from child/parent to friend/parent. Recently, there have been more and more times where Bryce and I have had meaningful conversations about adult things. I have turned to him for some advice. My son has inherited the uncanny ability from my dad to calm me during times of stress.

He doesn't worry about much, and on several occasions he has told me, "Don't worry about it, Mom. Let it go. It's all going to work out. It'll be fine." My son has always been an "old soul," wise beyond his years. And just like that, in a blink of an eye, he has grown into a smart, confident, capable, and wise young man.

One particular time where my dad helped me through a difficult period was when I was in high school. This instance stands out because it ended up being one of the best times of my life even though it was challenging. I was a senior and had just begun dating the person who would eventually become my husband. In typical teenage girl fashion, and we all know how cruel kids, especially teenagers, can be, some untrue and hurtful rumors were started about me. The long and the short of it was that half the girls in my grade ignored me, spread those rumors, and ostracized me. I dreaded going to school. I came home and cried about how they were treating me. I felt so alone at times.

One night, my dad came to my room and sat next to me. I was lying on my bed, probably looking at a *Teen Beat* magazine, reading an article about Madonna, and he laid his hand over mine and said, "You know, the fact that all of those people are spending so much time talking about you, you should feel honored. They have nothing better to do than to spend all of their time thinking and talking about you. Mean, yes. However, it won't be long before they find someone else to spend their time on. This too shall pass."

I thought about that for a moment, and he was absolutely right. He put his arm around me and pulled me close, saying, "I know this seems like the most important thing going on in your life, and for right now, it is. But you'll look back on this one day and realize it wasn't all that. I promise. This...will...pass."

Recalling this memory, as a parent, I can imagine how that must have killed him to see me go through something so hurtful.

Yet, he didn't show it. He showed me how to be strong, how to realize that this was just a moment in the grand scheme of things, and this wouldn't be the end of my world.

When it came to stressful situations, I would describe my dad as Cool Hand Luke. He always had the uncanny ability to ease my mind. No matter what I was stressing about, worrying, or obsessing about, he always, *always* comforted me and made me feel better.

When most kids are sick, they want their moms. For me, it was my dad. He'd give me my medicine, tuck me in, get my ginger ale, toast, Saltine crackers, and chicken noodle soup. He would feel my head, take my temperature. He comforted me. Don't get me wrong, my mom did those things too, but he just had a way about him that made me feel like I was going to be okay. My mom was an anxious person. She always panicked and worried about everything obsessively. I know she did the best she could.

I had the most unfortunate experience of getting chicken pox when I was 15. From my understanding, the older you are when you get chicken pox, the worse it is. I ran a 104-degree temperature for over a week. I remember being drenched in sweat yet shivering, feeling like I was freezing. I was dressed in my winter pajamas, and more than one heavy winter blanket covered me. The high fever caused me to have these weird, delirious dreams. My dad would soak my feet in cold water and put a cold, wet washcloth on my head. On more than one occasion, I awoke to him feeling my forehead and checking my fever. He would make me eat little things like a scrambled egg or a piece of toast and always made sure I was drinking to stay hydrated. At one point, my fever got so high that my dad stripped me down to my undies and soaked me in a cool bath. He never left my side. My fever finally broke. Besides being covered in pox and itching from head to toe, I was on the road to feeling better.

When I was really little, maybe four or five, on several occasions, no matter how tired he was when he got home from work, he was willing to play a game with me. One of my favorites was the Memory Game. It was a card game where the cards had pictures on them. You would mix them, lay them face down, and then try to pair the pictures, remembering where the matching card was. We would sit on the dark forest green carpet that covered our living room floor. I would turn the box over as the cards fell out. I was given the task of mixing them, turning them face down, and spreading them out on the floor. We played that game several times and I loved every minute of it, probably because I won most of the time. Come to think of it, my dad probably let me win.

I think it's safe to say that any man who is a father to a little girl has had the wonderful opportunity of getting their hair and make-up done. I clearly remember putting about a dozen or so colorful barrettes in my dad's hair and tinting his cheeks with a bright, bubble gum pink blush. I painted his lips a gaudy color of red, and, of course, I finished the entire makeover with the most hideous shade of powder blue eye shadow. What a trooper my dad was, and to all the other dads out there who endured this treatment, you're the best, and your little girl or girls will remember these moments fondly.

Another memory relates to math. How many of us love math? I don't know the numbers (literally), but I do not! I have a profound fear of the subject. I'm sure I am in good company. My fear and hatred of math started in the third grade, the year we learned our multiplication tables. I struggled with numbers. I was failing math and the one-minute, three-minute, and five-minute tests we had to take. I hated it and I failed every single one of them!

Being the involved parent he was, my dad was well aware of my math troubles. One day he brought this huge piece of black slate home from work with him. It was about three feet by eight feet long. He placed it in our spare room downstairs. This room was a little out of the way and afforded us the chance to work on my math homework without any interruptions. Without fail, every day after dinner for months and months and months, we went downstairs and practiced the multiplication tables from 0 through 12. Through all of my hesitation, frustration, begging, and pleading to take a day off, we stuck with it and it paid off. Today I am a human calculator when it comes to multiplying. There were several occasions where I was in tears, tired from the repetitive practicing. My dad didn't waiver one bit. Those tears were useless to him. I went from failing to getting an A on my multiplication tables! I learned to love those one-minute, three-minute, and five-minute tests. Dad never gave up on me and believed I could do it.

The town I grew up in, Ogdensburg, New Jersey, is a very old, tiny, quaint town. It was a wonderful country place to grow up. Mountains, rolling hills, and winding country roads bordered uneven yet beautiful rock walls built by generations past. Ponds perfect for cooling off in the summer or ice skating in the winter were scattered everywhere. The local landscape included open fields with rows of corn and hay, apple orchards, farms, and pastures with dairy cows. Winters were cold with lots of snow. Summers were about three months long and filled with hot, humid days. In fall, the most vibrant, gorgeous colors covered the foliage as the trees changed and displayed their bright oranges, yellows, and reds of the season.

Thomas Edison built and oversaw the operations of the zinc mine in Ogdensburg from 1889 to 1900. That's a little historic tidbit that only locals know. If you visit there today, you'll find a small museum dedicated to the zinc mine, Thomas Edison, and the people who worked the mine. Some of those miners lived in the mountains behind our house. On several occasions, my dad and I hiked through those mountains. When we were diligent enough and trekked to the top of the mountain, we reached, as we locals called it, "Eagle's Head," a large, flat rock that sat at the peak. Sitting on that boulder, we could see Ogdensburg and the small towns to the left and right of ours. The view was and still is breathtaking.

On one of our hikes, we got lucky and stumbled upon the remains of some of those miners' houses. Made of wood with a stone and mortar foundation, these two-story homes were in serious disrepair and decay. We knew it was not safe to try the weathered, dilapidated stairs. In one house we found several pop bottles dated from decades gone by, dishes, and cups. Some furniture remained, a kitchen table and rocking chair that wasn't in bad shape. In another house, I distinctly remember a tub made of white porcelain, now riddled with chips from age and the elements, and large, tarnished bear claw feet. It was beautiful. I recall thinking, "How the heck did they get this heavy tub up this mountain?"

We had a way of finding old, abandoned houses. Whenever we stumbled upon these little treasures, I would find myself constantly thinking about the family who lived there and wondering how they ended up there? How many of them were there? Who were they? What was their day like? What did they do? Did they own any of the surrounding property? Did a loved one die in that house? Were there any family members buried on the property? Were family members still living somewhere locally? What were their Christmases, birthdays, and celebrations like?

Fast forward a few decades later, and that love and curiosity for old, abandoned houses still drives me to occasionally pull over while I'm driving, get out, and approach a house that looks perfect for meandering through. Of course, I check the doors and windows, but have been known to shimmy a lock or two. I am absolutely fascinated with old dwellings that once were full of life, love, sound, and memories. As I walk through the halls and rooms that at one time were filled of furniture, life, and trinkets, I look at the once bright walls now covered in chipped paint or the remnants of floral patterned wallpaper that is now faded and peeling. Hardwood floors that someone painstakingly took the time to cut, sand, lay, and stain were once new and gleaming and now are weathered, warped, and worn. Tattered and frayed curtains that shaded the sun-filled rooms have turned a dingy gray, but some time ago they brightened the space in vibrant peach, pink, or green. The cabinetry in the kitchen, old and broken at the hinges, held canned goods and dinner plates in days long past. I imagine the family enjoying meals and having discussions as they ate from that china. I view the antiquated appliances that were once in style and functioning. I caress the worn banisters that line the crumbling staircase where countless hands had steadied those on the way up and down those stairs—on their way to work, school, church, family gatherings and holidays, and even to bed at the end of a long day. I wonder what the sunset looked like sitting on the front porch where the family adjourned after a long day. What did they talk about? What stories did they share? Did they enjoy a cup of coffee, a glass of wine, beer, or iced tea? Perhaps the family's homemade libation?

So much history—I truly wished those walls could talk. I believe that if my dad never introduced me to those old, abandoned houses way back when, I wouldn't have the obsessive love, curiosity, and respect for them that still burns deep within me today. I also have a love of history, particularly the time period of the mid-1800s to the turn of the century. He opened my eyes and my mind to always think. Look at what's in front of you, but think about what came before you and what is yet to be.

Throughout my childhood, we also took some awesome family trips. My favorite and by far the most memorable was our first trip to Florida. I was four years old at the time, and I clearly recall that trip like it was yesterday. We packed up our two-door 1972 forest green Ford Pinto. My parents put my old crib mattress in the back, and I slept on that mattress for hours at a time as we made our way from state to state, getting closer and closer to Florida.

That little car was jam-packed with suitcases, beach stuff, snacks, and, of course, a large thermos of hot coffee for my dad. At that time, Route 95 was still under construction, so we spent most of our time traveling on secondary roads at the modest speed of 35 mph. Needless to say, it took us a few days to get to our destination. If memory serves me, it took three days to finally cross the Georgia border into Florida. I clearly remember leaving each state. As each state welcomed us, my excitement grew. Along the way, we would make pit stops at each state's welcome center. I recall watching out the windows as we passed stores, houses, open fields, abandoned little farmhouses and recollect the feeling of the air getting warmer and warmer the farther south we traveled. The smell of the air and the humidity changed too. I distinctly remember the odor of the paper mill plants as soon as we hit North Carolina. To this day, a whiff of anything that slightly resembles that smell, and I am instantly brought back to that first trip to Florida.

We stopped at one hotel on Route 95 South. If memory serves me, I believe back in the day it was a Howard Johnson's.

I recall playing on their awesome jungle gym right next to the pool for hours at a time. The hotel sat on the south side of Route 95. The building remains today, but it is no longer in business. The jungle gym no longer displays the bright blues, yellows, and reds of all those years ago. It is corroded and heavily rusted. The hotel sits vacant now, its restaurant and rooms empty. The same orange curtains still cover the windows, but they are faded and torn. The pool is simply a blue concrete hole in the ground. The trees are overgrown and there are tall weeds everywhere. The blacktop entrance and parking lot has cracks woven throughout, and weeds grow in them as well. The roof on the hotel is starting to collapse. Yet, every time my kids and I happen to pass that hotel in our travels, I point it out, and, just as I'm about to tell them I played on that jungle gym years ago, they stop me and say, "Yes, mom, we know. You stopped there when you were a little girl and played on that jungle gym." I guess I have mentioned it to them once or twice.

Traveling down Route 95, there are several rest stops along the way. We would frequent these little areas whenever we could. These pit stops would serve as a potty break, time to walk around and stretch our legs, and an opportunity for my dad to take a quick nap before continuing toward our destination. The rest stop in Florida is just over the Georgia/Florida line and is famous for serving a small cup of freshly-squeezed orange juice to all who visit. To this day, they carry on that tradition. My dad didn't know it at the time, but all of these little things that to most would seem insignificant, I hold so close and dear to my heart. My heart and my mind are full of thousands and thousands of memories, large and small, that my dad was such a huge part of. These made an impact on me as a child and as an adult. I hope that anyone reading this is able to think back and recall with fondness, smiles, and love the little moments their parents gave them.

Florida holds many, many, special memories for me. We have family that lives there on both coasts. Throughout the years, we visited several times. The Gulf Coast was my favorite. I was four the first time I went to Disney World. I vividly recall the rides, the smell of hot dogs and popcorn, and the bustle of the crowds. I was excited to see all of the rides and the lines of people patiently waiting their turn. Parents pushed strollers packed full of goodies from the park. I clearly recall the outfit I wore, the warmth of the sun, the exhilaration of the day.

Back in the day, we didn't have to sign up or check for the designated areas in the park where the Disney characters or princesses would be for you to visit them. They would be casually walking throughout the park, and you could easily just walk up to any one of them and get your picture taken without waiting. What child would not love walking through Cinderella's Castle upon entering the park?! How wonderful to feel the dark coolness of the tunnel through the castle that leads into the park. It was lined with little shops where we could buy our memorabilia upon arriving or on the way out.

I went on the Peter Pan ride with my dad, flying overhead, just like Peter Pan, above the miniature city that was lit up below us. That ride was dark too, and I remember holding on to my dad for dear life. It was just a little too dim and shadowy for my four-year-old self. Captain Hook was especially scary to me at the time.

It's a Small World was my mom's favorite ride. It consisted of sitting in a canoe-style boat with about a dozen or so other thrill seekers as the canoe casually glided through the ride, passing through each country. Figures of children dressed in their country's finest sang in their native language, "It's a Small World." There was no other way to describe it than a feel-good ride. No one could leave that ride in a bad mood.

Jiminy Cricket was always my favorite Disney character, but he was nowhere to be found at the park. Like every other parent, mine considered photo ops of their child of great importance. My mom thought it would be a good idea to take pictures with the Seven Dwarfs. Speaking for myself, seven short, stout men with incredibly large heads who were barely taller than me, some with scowls on their faces, scared the crap out of me. I took one look at that motley crew and said, "No way!" Well, that wouldn't do for my mom. She started raising her voice at me, pointing and demanding that I stand next to one of them and take a picture. I resisted, but, thanks to my mother's nagging, I gave in. The result: a picture of me with a hesitant, fearful, not happy to be doing this look on my face, never looking at them or the camera, head down, waiting for that awkward moment to end. That picture and memory is etched in my mind and is also in one of our family photo albums.

However, karma gave my mom a little *nudge*. Somewhere in the park, there was a pen that housed baby goats and adolescents. They were adorable! They'd run over to and around visitors, hopping joyfully. If they stood still long enough, you could pet them. A few of them were daring enough to take a slight nibble at the fabric of the clothes we were wearing. Some of the goats were curious enough to stand on their hind legs and check out the people. Well, a few of them found my mother quite interesting. Not one, not two, but at least three or four jumped up on my mom. My mother's typical response to animals jumping on her was to flail her arms, shooing them away.

"Get down! Get down! Stop it! Get away!" she kept demanding as her voice grew louder and more intense. As her annoyance and resistance grew, I stood at a distance watching, finding the entire scene quite enjoyable!

Certain things about that trip definitely stand out in my memory. First and most obvious was spending the entire day at

Disney. Unfortunately, when we got back to our hotel that night, my parents realized I had a severe case of sunburn. I was so bad off they had to cut my clothes off me because I was too sore to lift my arms over my head. The other definitive memory was an orange grove located along the main road from Disney to our hotel. We had never seen an orange orchard before, so, of course, it piqued our interest, and we had to stop and check it out. How many chances do Northerners from New Jersey get to pick fresh, ripe oranges? Without hesitation, we had to take just a few. If memory serves me, of course I was only four, but they were nearly impossible to pick and pull off those trees! We have a picture of my little self working as hard as I could to free an orange from a branch. I could barely fit my small hands around that piece of fruit. I held on tightly and twisted, turned and pulled as hard as I could, but that branch was not willing to let the orange go. Finally, with my dad's help, we were able to bring three oranges back to the hotel with us.

One more thing that stands out in my memory was my *favorite* outfit that I wore several times on our trip: little white sandals, lavender and daisy printed shorts that were frayed at the ends, socks that folded over at the ankle and were edged in lace, a lavender shirt, and my hair always in two ponytails on each side of my head. Purple, particularly a light shade of it was and still is my favorite color. My other lasting loves from that trip were palm trees and Spanish moss. Anyone who knows me is aware that even today I have an obsession with palm trees and Spanish moss!

As a little girl, there were so many things I wished for—whether for Christmas, my birthday, or no special occasion at all. The one treasure I really wanted was a dollhouse. The Sears Christmas catalog that came out every year had a section that featured dollhouses. I would stare at those pictures, imagining how I would decorate those tiny rooms. I loved those miniature pieces of furniture, dressers that had miniscule golden knobs and working drawers, kitchen utensils, cups, plates, spoons, frying pans, curtains, area rugs, pictures, adorable lamps with shades that had fringes on them, and little decorative plants. When I was about 10, my dad would come home from work, and after dinner he would lock himself in our guest bedroom. For months, night after night, he would retire to that room, spending hours working, many times way past my bedtime. A bright, yellow glow shone from underneath the door. Sounds of brush strokes on wood, hammering and sanding, and the occasional cuss word came from that room as well. Strong vapors of glue, varnish, and paint wafted through the other rooms in the house. I was given strict orders by my father that I was never to go into that room. I was absolutely forbidden.

About six months later on a cold, crisp, snowy morning, the excitement and anticipation of Christmas and all of those wonderful, colorfully wrapped boxes topped with bows and filled with surprises, just waiting to be opened, woke me early. I bounced out of bed and made my way to the living room. Our Christmas tree stood in the far corner, decorated in colorful lights, red garland, and the prettiest of decorations that my dad and I made ourselves over the years. The tree was topped with a softly lit angel that was dressed in white and had feathers for wings. Off to the side of our Christmas tree, there was something huge that was covered by a large bed sheet. It stood about three feet high and three feet wide. A picture in one of our family albums captures the moment I pulled away that sheet and uncovered my new dollhouse. I was dressed in yellow footie pajamas, my hair a mess, my eyes wide, and a huge smile exposing a mixture of adult and baby teeth. My face expressed a look of surprise and excitement. As I pulled away the sheet, all the intricate work and amount of time my dad spent on the dollhouse amazed me.

My dollhouse was three stories high, painted in a white stucco with dark wood trim. Each window had a flower box. There was a balcony off the third-story den with working French doors. The first two stories on the left side of the house had large bay windows. The first floor displayed the living room, dining room, and kitchen. A staircase covered in carpeting and adorable molded banisters led to the second story, which had two bedrooms. Another set of staircases led to the third story, where the master bedroom, bathroom, and den were. Each room in the dollhouse was trimmed and had crown molding. Each door had little hinges and doorknobs. The front door actually worked with an itty-bitty key. My dad spent almost a year putting that house together by hand. He sanded, painted, and glued every tiny piece of that house. He even made a few pieces of furniture including beds, dressers, nightstands, and side tables for the living room, even the sink for the kitchen, and a little hanging shelf, a place to put the dinner plates. I didn't know it at the time, but he built that dollhouse when his eyesight had started to decline. I played with it for years. I had a family of four, a mom and dad, a son and daughter. I spent hours decorating it, painting the walls, making tiny decorative pillows. I would save my money, and my dad would occasionally take me to a little craft store in a town about 20 minutes from our house. What a treat that was! I would've spent all day in that store, looking at all the pieces of tiny furniture and accessories. They even had working lamps, chandeliers, and lights to hang outside of the house. It was all so wonderful, and I wanted to buy all of it.

I passed my dollhouse down to my daughter, and she has started the task of re-decorating it. She doesn't much like the flowered patterned couch, the bright pink walls in the girl's room, or the green carpeting in the living room.

Something else that remains from my childhood is the importance of respect, a value my dad always held in high regard. From my dad's perspective, respect had to be earned regardless of who you were. Respect was not demanded, bought, or forced. Once earned, according to my dad, respect took work to maintain and was hard to regain if lost. As long as I can remember, my dad always said, "You respect me; I'll respect you."

As I entered my teen years, the subject of dating, parties, and curfews became a small obstacle for us. The big thing about dating for my dad was respecting myself. He always told me, drilled it into me, "Respect yourself and those that matter will too." I dated with those words in mind, and they proved to be so very true. Most of the boys and young men I dated respected me. There were one or two who didn't, and when I stood my ground on respecting myself, they walked. It hurt for that moment, but I was glad they walked out of my life. To this day, I have no regrets and feel proud that I valued myself enough not to sell out on my personal principles.

Curfews were a hot-button topic at first. But we established some guidelines, and with every party those boundaries were set. I respected my dad's wishes, and he returned that respect by allowing me to stay out later on occasions when I asked. We had an understanding when it came to curfews. I was not to come home one hour later, five minutes after, or even one minute after the deadline he had set. I was to be home *at* the appointed time. However, if for any reason, I felt unsafe or couldn't get home in time for my curfew, I could call my dad, no questions asked, and he would come and get me. We followed these guidelines the entire time I was in high school and even when I returned home for visits between college breaks. His rule: "When in Rome, do as the Romans do." Regardless of how old I was, as long as I lived under his roof, I followed his rules.

Patience was another thing my dad had in abundance when it came to children. He often said, "I have patience with children because they don't know any better. I don't with adults because they should." Throughout the years, I heard my dad say this a hundred times. When it came to his interactions with children, he had all the patience in the world. He didn't fly off the handle, get easily frustrated, or yell. However, disobey him, disrespect him, make the same mistake over and over, and, yes, he would yell and you *would* be disciplined!

He always loved spending time with kids just doing whatever. He played all sorts of games from board games to flashlight tag in the middle of summer with the kids that lived on our street. He was known to take some of the boys in the neighborhood fishing or hunting. When the kids asked him about something, he did not just talk to them; he showed them. He took his time. My dad had this softness about him when he interacted with children. His voice lowered and became gentle. He explained and described things in detail. You could see those little gears working in that young mind; he saw it too, and I think that was satisfying for him. He always said, "Children are like sponges; make sure what they're soaking up is good."

These were the little things we assume all parents teach. He taught me how to ride my first bike, first with training wheels and then without. He taught me how to catch fish. He showed me how to cook. He taught me how to hit a ball and catch for my first season in softball. He showed me how to tie my shoes and how to drive a car. He explained how to write checks and helped me open my first savings account. He helped me do my taxes those first few years.

After getting through those agonizing driver's education classes, I got so excited about getting behind the wheel. I finally felt free from the chains of being bound by my parents having to drive me everywhere. I could go hang out with friends or meet them at a party or a movie. I could spend time with my boyfriend!

As luck would have it, my driver's test to get my license was the day after my junior prom. This scene plays out in my mind like it happened yesterday. About an hour before my date and my friends with their dates were due to arrive, I was all dressed and ready for the prom. I'd done my hair and makeup and put on my prom dress and shoes. Since we had the time, my dad thought it would be the perfect opportunity to practice my driving skills, so he strategically placed two garbage cans on the street in front of our house. We got into our Ford Fairmont; I started the car and backed down and out of our driveway. For the next hour, I practiced driving, parallel parking, and how to do a K-turn. Finally, I passed my dad's driving test with flying colors.

Another vivid memory from my teens relates to the movie *Jaws*. Even today, whenever *Jaws* is playing on any station, I immediately stop what I'm doing and watch. If you asked my kids what their mom's favorite movie is, while rolling their eyes as if to say, "Are you kidding me," in unison, they would say, "*Jaws!*" They would tell you that my dad took me to Newton Movie Theatre to see *Jaws* when I was all of nine years old. I remember watching with intent, wonder, and a little fear. I hung on to my dad's arm in that dark theatre, occasionally snacking on popcorn and sipping soda. I think we can all collectively agree that the line, "You're gonna need a bigger boat," is something we can all recite.

That movie made an impression on me, good and bad. I already had a wonder and curiosity about the ocean and the sea life that lives deep below the surface. I think my dad sensed my apprehension after watching the movie, and, in his typical jokester fashion, he couldn't pass up an opportunity to have a little fun with me that night. When we got home, I got ready for bed, doing the usual routine of putting on my PJs, brushing my teeth, and going to the bathroom. As I sat on the toilet, performing my nightly ritual, my dad stood on the other side of the bathroom door, and softly in his deep voice hummed the theme to *Jaws*: "Da-Da, Da-Da, Da-Da, Da-Da." I don't think I really *sat* on the toilet for a few weeks after that, and, when I did use the bathroom, I looked down into the toilet, making sure nothing made its way out and up from the sewers to grab me by the ass.

We saw a lot of other movies together including the original *Star Wars*. I remember standing in a line that wrapped around the building and into the parking lot to go see that movie. We both loved that film and the time we spent together watching it.

Clash of the Titans, starring a young and good-looking Harry Hamlin, kick-started my interest in Greek mythology. I loved the characters, the love story, and the theme of good conquering evil, and thought the special effects of that day were awesome. My favorite character was Medusa, who had snakes for hair, a half-snake, half-human body that creepily slithered along, and a wicked look as she waited for her next victim.

Richard Flusz was not only an amazing father but the best papa any grandchild would be so blessed to have—a fact my kids will attest to. Being an only child, my two children were the only grandkids my parents had. Both of my parents were wonderful grandparents to my children. My dad was hands-on with me and with my kids. He displayed the same kind of patience and excitement for learning with my kids that he had with me and the many kids that grew up in our neighborhood. If anyone were to sit down with my kids and ask them what they think of their papa, they would relate countless memories of meandering trips for a day or a week and all the things he shared with them and taught them that they will never forget. Of course, they also would tell you about several one-liners that made them laugh or embarrassed them. They still smile and shake their heads about some of those and say, "That's my papa."

My daughter recently had the stressful, arduous, and adult task of deciding between two colleges that had awarded her substantial scholarships. She liked both schools, Pratt in NYC and MICA in Baltimore, Maryland. Location and the left-over amount she would be responsible for paying were the two major factors in her decision making. After weeks of weighing the pros and cons, she chose MICA.

During the decision process, she and I got into some heated discussions about her choice. As a parent and an adult who has a great deal more real-life experience than her, I tried to help her understand the magnitude of the loan amount she would be taking on for her education. We also discussed that most do not come out of college and find their high-paying, dream job. She equated that statement with me not believing in her or her talents. I truly believe my daughter has a gift, and she will be very successful. However, I know how competitive and rough it is in the real world, and the cost of living combined with an outrageous student loan would put her behind the eight ball after graduation.

After she made her decision and the heat of our discussions and stress subsided, she said to me, "There's only one person in my life I truly know believes in me: Papa. Papa never lies, never tells people things they *want* to hear, or says things just to make people happy. Papa always says it like he sees it. Ever since I was a little girl, Papa has always said, 'Little girl, you are so talented. Remember me when you make it big.'"

My dad became a father figure to both of my kids, especially my son. He spent time with them, taught them, listened to and shared with them. I have this adorable picture of my dad and my son. Bryce was about a year and a half the first time my dad took him fishing. Nineteen years later, my son loves fishing and has a collection of rods, reels, and tackle. My dad also introduced him to history, war, and guns. He always believed it was okay for kids to watch factual war movies. My dad was always open and honest and willing to discuss the good and the bad of our past. A well of knowledge when it came to world war history, he could talk for hours if someone was patient and willing to listen and discuss. Conversations with my dad always left us more knowledgeable and, at times, made us question what we thought we knew.

Chapter 4: That Reminds Me...

There are certain things that stand out in my mind about my dad. No matter how old I get or where I am, those things instantly take me back to a moment in time. These priceless reminders will forever bring my dad to mind.

First and foremost, the smell of coffee evokes countless memories of Dad. The man *loved* his coffee. May parents had this stainless-steel percolator for at least 20 years. After so many years of use, the stained inside no longer resembled the shiny interior it had decades earlier. My dad must have drunk 12 to 14 cups of coffee a day—no joke.

Fishing always conjures up memories of my dad. From the stories my aunt and my cousin have told me, my grandfather was the one who instilled the love of fishing in my dad. The only photo my dad had of his father pictured him fishing. I was always curious about the man in that black and white picture. He wasn't a tall man, maybe about 5' 7". His dark hair was balding, and a fat cigar hung from the corner of his mouth. He was squinting from the sun, and he wore loose fitting jeans with a belt and a white T-shirt. Beside him in the photo, my father stood proudly displaying a large fish that I'm assuming he caught. My dad said the fish was most likely a red drum he caught off the coast of the Jersey shore.

The smell of cigarette smoke summons a vision of my dad, who smoked since he was 13. Unfortunately, cigarettes were the culprit behind my father's cancer. Winston Red 100s were his favorites. He continued to smoke even after his diagnosis. But I thought, "Why stop him or give him grief about it? He's living out the rest of his days on his terms, and I respect him for that."

My dad loved deep, dark forest green. Not a mint green, fern, juniper, lime, or pear shade of green but instead the deepest shade of pine or avocado you can imagine. Our first family car, the infamous Ford Pinto, was that avocado green. Of course, it had that hard, cold vinyl interior in the same shade. Our house was dark green and so was our carpet. Green is not my favorite color, and I don't have a stitch of it in my home today; too much of it in my childhood was more than enough for me.

Kiffles, otherwise known as Hungarian Christmas cookies, call so many memories to mind. Every year my dad carried out the tradition that began with my great grandmother of baking a big batch of Kiffles for Christmas. To make these scrumptious, light, buttery, flaky, thin pastries filled with crushed walnuts, minced apricots, or prunes, he would cut the dough into small squares with two opposite edges folded over the filling. When they come out of the oven, warm and baked to a light golden-brown, he gently dusted them with powdered sugar. The tartness of the filling complimented the buttery-sweetness of the pastry. Yum! These were a delicious treat we all looked forward to around the holidays. After I had kids, baking these cookies became a tradition for my family as well. First my son Bryce would make them with my dad, and then, when he got older, Carleigh took over the tradition. Together, they would make at least three or four dozen of these tasty treats, which would only last a day or two. Even my kids' friends enjoyed them.

Butter was my dad's go-to spread for *everything*. He put it on toast, sandwiches, all vegetables, pasta, rice, oatmeal. I distinctly remember sitting around the kitchen table, waiting for my mom to put the finishing touches on dinner. My dad would be sitting across from me reading a book while snacking on butter. Without taking his eyes off the page he was reading, he would take the tip of a butter knife, cut little slivers of butter, and slide it off on his tongue, enjoying the sensation of its creaminess melting in his mouth. Sliver after sliver after sliver. We kept a stick of butter on a dish, never refrigerated, because my dad always wanted his butter soft, ready to spread on any available piece of food. As I wrote the memoir, he had 10 pounds of butter in his refrigerator!

My dad collected coins for years and amassed quite an extensive collection—old coins, new coins, silver, copper, gold, silver dollars, wheat pennies, buffalo nickels, special minted coins, bicentennial coins, lots of two-dollar bills. He had dozens and dozens of coin holders, all carefully labeled, with each coin placed strategically in a specific slot according to how my dad categorized them. Just the other day, I was cleaning his bedroom and found a little locker, stocked full of coins of all types. Besides collecting coins for their value, we also rolled coins and cashed them in. What was always exciting for me was saving all of that extra change until our piggy bank was full. We would start by first separating them into piles of pennies, nickels, dimes and quarters. We spent hours sitting on our living room floor, painstakingly rolling them. At the time, if we rolled fifty dollars' worth of coins, I thought we were rich! Fifty dollars is a lot to an eight-year-old.

I will always, always think of my dad whenever I hear the theme to the TV show *The Lone Ranger* but not for reasons one might think. I recall countless times when my dad sat at the kitchen table, for a host of different reasons, tapping his fingers to the theme to *The Lone Ranger*. The William Tell Overture, the music that accompanied the opening credits, was perfect to strum your fingers to and make the tapping sound like the building of that theme song. I heard him strum his fingers to that tune over and over again until, without realizing it, I picked up the ability to tap out the theme to *The Lone Ranger* myself. Without practice, I just one day started doing it. I've caught myself several times tapping it. It may seem silly, but that's something that sticks in my mind as a memory of my dad and of my childhood.

As weird as it sounds, flannel shirts remind me of my dad. He was never been one to dress up for any occasion. Flannel shirts have been his go-to fashion for as long as I can remember. Years ago, he wore them until they were worn, paper thin, stained, and ripped. My mom and dad argued frequently about retiring those shirts. She would sneak them into the garbage, and he would pull them out and hold onto them. About 30 flannel shirts still hung in his closest at the moment I wrote this.

Another reminder of my father was nasal spray. Readers may well think to themselves, "What the heck is this chick going to write about pertaining to nasal spray? Weirdo." Well, my dad used nasal spray *every* day. Several times throughout the day, I heard a spray, snort, and inhale. Nasal spray bottles were scattered throughout the house. They could be found in my parents' bedroom, on my dad's nightstand, in the kitchen, bathroom, and on the desk in his office. Years ago, one time when he had a cold, my dad needed nasal spray, and he got addicted to it and continued to use it all these years.

Whenever a John Wayne movie comes on, I can't help thinking of my dad. He was a huge fan of The Duke and watched every movie he ever made a dozen times each. He could recite the lines in almost every scene. While he loved John Wayne's work, he also admired the man and considered him a true American, no nonsense, confident yet humble, and proud of his country.

Chilton books bring back memories of my dad. We had several Chilton auto repair books scattered around the house. As a self-taught auto mechanic, my dad loved these how-to-fix-it manuals for every make, model, and year of any car. I've always been so very proud of him for teaching himself to become a mechanic. He learned everything he needed to know by trying, failing, reading, learning, trying again, and succeeding (most of the time). He knew how to fix a "four-banger" as he called them (cars with four cylinders). V-sixes, no problem. V-eights, bring it. This little blonde knows something about cars too. By the time I purchased my first car at the age of 22, I was changing my own oil and checking the fluids and spark plugs, replacing windshield wipers, checking my brake pads and knowing, by checking the depth of them and their wear and tear, when it was time to replace them. I know what the rotors are, what they look like, and what purpose they serve.

My dad taught me to be in tune with the sounds and feel, the vibrations, etc. of my car when I drive. I can tell by the feel in the steering wheel and the brake pedal whether I need a tire rotation, a balance, or if there's an issue with my brakes or rotors. I know a little about the functioning that the alternator and the starter each serve. Front and rear mounts, yep, I know a little something about them too and what it feels like to drive a car when I have a problem with one. I even had the opportunity to learn how to repair the V6 transmission in our Ford Fairmont. It wasn't the ideal way to spend Friday and Saturday nights as a senior in high school, but I learned a lot that winter.

The smell of an auto mechanic's garage brings my dad to mind every time. The smell of oil, transmission fluid, grease, metal, the dust, and the mustiness remind me of my dad. The sound of the drills and air guns still echo in my memory. I've never known my dad to have truly clean hands. He loved to work with his hands. From the stories he shared with me about his childhood, in his younger days, he was always taking things apart. This drove my grandmother crazy because often he wouldn't be able to put those things completely back together in any kind of working fashion. Growing up, I loved the fact that he was a hardcore, blue collar, working class man. He never felt any job was beneath him. As long as he earned a living and provided for his family, he felt proud of the work he did. Several times through the years, he worked more than one job to provide for us and make sure he was putting money away for me to go to college.

Another reminder of my dad comes in the form of a bird: the robin red breast. Anytime my dad would see a robin, he would say, "Spring is coming; the robins are out." As early as January, if he saw a robin, according to him that meant spring was right around the corner. Never a person who enjoyed the cold or snow, spring was always his favorite season. Every year, once the final leaf dropped from the trees and fall turned into winter, he had horrible cabin fever. He complained about the gray, dreary, cold New Jersey days of winter and begged for spring. Thanks to him, I have that same dislike for the winter and all it brings, longing for the days of spring with the same intensity he had. Now, whenever I see a robin hopping along, searching for its lunch, I smile and warmly and lovingly think of my dad. Till the day I take my last breath, I will think of my dad whenever I see these beautiful birds.

Classical music fondly reminds me of my dad. Beethoven, Bach, Chopin, Tchaikovsky—my dad knew them all and loved their music. It's hard for me to imagine that a long time ago, sometime in the early 1950s, my dad was this rebellious, slick-haired, smoking, smart-mouthed, James Dean looking teenager. Well, I can envision the smart-mouth, somewhat rebellious part, but to think that this strict disciplinarian of a man considered the popular music of his era and classical music, as he put it, "the only good music worth listening to. The rest is crap," he would say. Riding in the car with my dad, we would only listen to classical music. He had dozens of CDs of the stuff. As a result of being hard of hearing, he liked to listen to it with the speakers booming. He also loved to play the Trans-Siberian Orchestra's music every Christmas.

My generation grew up watching Warner Brothers Looney Tunes cartoons. Without knowing it at the time, we were exposed to classical music as it played in the background while Bugs Bunny was outsmarting Daffy Duck or the Road Runner stuck it to Wile E. Coyote. My dad often enjoyed watching these cartoons with me. Whenever we were viewing an episode that just happened to have classical music in the background, he would quiz me. "What's the name of that piece they're playing? Who's the composer?" I had to hope I got the answer right, or I would soon get re-educated—snore!

A few weekends ago, my boyfriend and I were experiencing a beautiful afternoon at the beach, sharing a blanket on a sunny day. We sat there enjoying each other's company and listening to the sounds of people talking and splashing in the water and the roar of the waves crashing in the background. I happened to glance up at the sky, and there were two perfect, unbroken streaks of contrails above us. I smiled a big grin. Contrails are those white lines that appear in the sky behind a plane in flight. Thanks to my dad, my children and I know what they are!

Most of these reminders may seem odd to those who didn't know my dad. Why would I even mention them? It's all the little things that bring us closer to someone we love, especially after that loved one is no longer with us. We cling to these "little things," holding them close to our hearts. That keeps the ones we miss close to us.

Chapter 5: Young James Dean

My mom had this photo album. The cover was a navy blue with small, brightly colored flowers. This album held one of my favorite pictures of Dad. In the black and white photo, this young boy, maybe 10 or 12, was wearing jeans rolled up to above the ankles, a white, long-sleeved shirt, and sneakers that looked similar to white Converse. His dirty blond hair was flowing upward as if it was windy. His arms were flailing behind him. The expression on his face was one of pure excitement—eyes wide, mouth open. This snapshot captured the thrill of him doing something he shouldn't. That boy was my dad, and this picture showed him jumping off the second story of the house he grew up in. According to family members who knew him at that age, this photo perfectly portrayed the type of boy and young man he was.

Not a big man, only five feet, seven inches, he was always slender in his younger days, around 150 pounds *maybe*. However, according to my grandmother, he was one fat baby. He weighed over nine pounds when he was born, and, as my grandmother would say, "He was so fat as a baby, and it took him well over a year to walk."

My grandma, my cousin, my aunt (Dad's sister), and occasionally my dad would tell me stories about him when he was a boy and into young adulthood. My dad was close to his father, my grandpa. I've been told they did everything together. However, when my dad was 13, my grandpa died suddenly. This changed my dad's world and who he was forever. My aunt told me once, "When Dad died, a part of Richard died."

When my grandpa died, my grandmother had to become the main breadwinner. At the time, her sister, her nephew, and my dad, all lived in that house. My grandmother worked as a midwife or nurse. Dad would refer to both when he spoke about her. Needless to say, she wasn't home much. My dad's sister was nine years older than my dad. When he was 11, she was 20 and already married, starting her own family, so my dad was left to his own devices at times.

My dad was not just a troublemaker. He also had a love of and appreciation for animals and shared many stories of the pets he had as a boy. My favorite story, one he shared and retold frequently, was about two black crows he raised. I'm not sure how he found those eggs, but he incubated two crow's eggs until they hatched. He told me that once they had hatched, he would mash up earthworms with milk and feed them with an eyedropper. In Edison New Jersey, in the house where he grew up, my dad's bedroom was on the second story. These two crows he named appropriately Big One and Little One (for obvious reasons). He said that once the crows were old enough and could fly, early in the morning he would open his bedroom window, and they would fly out and do what crows do for the day. At dusk, they would return, and wait for him on his windowsill, spending the night in the makeshift nest my dad made for them, which consisted of a box with grass in it. This became their daily routine. My dad mentioned that, on more than one occasion, they took enjoyment in taunting the neighbor's cat. They would perch themselves on the clothesline in the backyard and just wait for that cat. Heckling and squawking, at the right time they would swoop down, just barely brushing the cat's back with their claws. They would also follow my dad down the street as he walked to his buddy Davie's house. Big One and Little One became quite fond of my dad and I guess considered him their parent. He had them for a few years until one day they just didn't return. My dad never knew what happened to them—whether they died or that neighbor with the cat got tired of their taunting. I have a photo of my dad feeding them. He sat on the stoop in the backyard, and alongside him a big crow and a small crow ate what he offered. My dad appeared to be rolling up pieces of bread into small balls in the picture. The crows appeared to be anxiously awaiting their treat.

He frequently spoke of a dog he had who was a collie mix. He never told me his name, but my dad mentioned that he went everywhere with that dog. Then one day, his four-legged companion was hit by a car. Decades later, my dad told me how much he missed that dog.

My dad also liked to hunt. I use the term loosely, because his idea of hunting was to use his slingshot to aim at one of the many squirrels displaying their acrobatics in the trees above. He wouldn't try to kill them needlessly. He liked eating them. My grandmother was truly a saint. If he happened to kill a squirrel, he would bring it home, and without a fuss my grandmother would clean my dad's kill and cook it for him. Quite a woman, I must say.

My grandmother shared a funny fact about my dad with me. When he was really little, around four or five, he had an imaginary friend he called Mr. Wiggly or Uncle Wiggles; I think he used the names interchangeably. My grandmother said he would go to the front door, open it, and welcome Mr. Wiggly in. He would carry on conversations, babbling about several topics that were of great importance to a boy of five. My grandmother commented that Richie was fully aware that Mr. Wiggly was there with him, listening intently. The rest of the family found this quite amusing.

I named this chapter Young James Dean because my dad was a rebel. In many pictures from the '50s, he wore his hair like they all did back then: a little longer on top, greased, and brushed to the side, resembling an Elvis swoop. In these photos, he had on a short-sleeved, white pocket T-shirt with jeans that were rolled up at the ankles, his white socks showing, and the popular sneakers of that day.

He started smoking when he was 11, and he rolled his pack of cigarettes in one of the sleeves of his T-shirt. He was also a troublemaker at school, never paying attention, cutting class and getting bad grades. I believe he was 16 when he quit high school. I'm not sure how he spent that time for those two years that he was not in high school, but I'm certain some of it was probably not legal.

He mentioned how he and his buddy Davie frequently drag raced. "Looking back on it now," he would say, "I'm damn lucky to be alive. We did some pretty stupid things back in the day."

Without prejudice, I have to say that my dad was an adorable boy and a handsome young man. As a boy, his hair was dirty blond, and he had big, brown eyes, dimples that were deep and adorable, and a devilish look to his smile. He did have somewhat big ears, but he was cute nonetheless. It makes me smile when I look at the pictures from those days, because he was smiling that devilish grin in every single one of them. He had this "if you only knew what I was thinking" look on his face. No matter what age he was, he was always up to something he shouldn't have been doing.

When I was about nine years old, I got a pair of ice skates for Christmas. On a typical, bitter cold winter day, my dad and I went ice skating at Heater's Pond, the little swimming hole in our town. During the summer, it was where everyone in town would go to swim. In the winter, it became the town's ice skating rink. This was also the location of the town's annual Christmas tree burning and bonfire, and it was a mere five-minute drive from our house. We parked the car and made our way to the frozen pond. We took off our winter boots and laced up our ice skates. All bundled up in winter coats, hats, earmuffs and gloves, my dad took my hand and carefully led me to the middle of the pond. Walking or skating on frozen water in the middle of the spot where we swam during the summer could be frightening. As we moved on the ice, it expanded, making a loud, pronounced cracking sound that echoed. We might even see cracks where we stepped. But in northwestern New Jersey, January was so cold that the ice might crack but not all the way through—at least not in the middle of the pond where the water was deep and the ice was thick.

We awkwardly walked on our skates to the middle of the pond. Then, my dad turned to face me. He took both my hands and gently pushed me away from him. There I unsteadily "skated" back a foot or two, slowly stopped, and just stood. He motioned with his hands, saying, "Okay, skate to me." I carefully pushed off my right foot, and there I was, skating. Right foot, left foot, right foot, left foot—that was my first lesson in ice skating. My dad was quite the ice skater in his younger days. I know this for a fact because his skating was quite impressive when he was teaching me. He taught me to skate forward and backward, how to stop and push off correctly, how to skate foot over foot and make figure eights. I never learned, but he knew how to do turns, the pirouettes that professionals do. He shared that one time in his younger days, he fell through the ice. He never told me how he made it out.

As a teenager and young man, his hair darkened. But those dimples and that devilish look made him quite handsome and gave him a certain amount of charm. I could see why my mom fell in love with him.

After dropping out of high school and doing God knows what for a year or two, he eventually smartened up and got his GED. After completing that, he enlisted in the military, the Marines. In 1958, at the age of 20, he was sent to Parris Island, South Carolina, for basic training. Some of the pictures of him in uniform are among of my favorites.

"I would eat more than I ever had, and I lost weight and got into the best shape of my life. I left as this skinny little kid, and I came home 25 pounds heavier, in shape, and quite handsome, I must say," he would say of those days, that same devilish grin on his face. If at any time he paid himself a compliment, it was always in jest with a bit of sarcasm.

Once on furlough during his time in the Marines, my dad and a few buddies thought it would be fun to spend the weekend in New Orleans. They hopped in a car from Parris Island and drove all night. He gave us little detail about how they spent their days drinking and walking the streets of the ever-so-flamboyant New Orleans. He mentioned that he enjoyed meeting and going out with a few ladies he met.

It was only about a year ago that he shared the fact that he had gotten arrested that weekend in New Orleans. The way he told it, he was heavily intoxicated and fell asleep. When a local New Orleans police officer tried to wake him, my dad got annoyed and told the man to leave him alone. I guess the officer attempted to wake my father again, and my dad punched him.

My dad woke up the next morning in jail. He said the cop was nice enough to offer him a cup of coffee despite the fact he had behaved like a smart ass.

My dad was always a private man, so any tidbit about his past or anything else he shared that allowed us a glimpse of the man he was, was a treat and a privilege. He never spoke much about the girls he dated. More than once he jokingly stated that I probably had a few brothers and sisters out there that I don't know about. "TMI, Dad, TMI."

Back in the day, drive-ins and burger joints were the places for young adults to hang out. The restaurant in *Happy Days* was exactly the kind of place where my parents and young adults in the 1950s spent their time, socializing with their friends. At the time, my mom was dating a close friend of my dad's. My dad was introduced to my mom and thought she was pretty. He made an arrangement with his buddy that he'd give his friend the number of the girl he was dating in exchange for my mom's number. The rest, as they say, is history.

My parents dated for about nine months and then got engaged. They were married on October 12, 1963. I was born on May 13, 1968. On that date, not only was I born but also the greatest dad ever was too.

Chapter 6: One Day at a Time

It's still hard to believe how much my life changed during those few weeks after my dad's diagnosis. We all go about our lives, minute by minute, day by day, week by week. Before we know it, weeks, months, seasons, and years have passed. As we go through our daily routines, we assume for the most part that the plans we make will happen and that people and places and things in our lives will still be there. All will remain the same. We also know but may not want to acknowledge that our lives can change on a dime. We have often read, heard, or spoken those words ourselves. And then it happens. Your life shifts and every single thing you know is tossed into the blender for you to drink, swallow, and deal with.

We had so many plans that now would never happen. I was consumed with work, money, kids, love, and life. Like most of us, I was focused on my future plans and goals and the people and places that were going to be part of those plans.

For the most part, over these last few weeks, my dad had mostly good days, sprinkled with some not-so-good moments. He was now on a regular schedule of morphine, which helped with his shortness of breath. He was also on oxygen, and there was a tank in his bedroom, his office, and the living room, the three rooms where he spent the most time. He took guaifenesin for his cough, which helped with the congestion in his lungs and wheezing. He slept *a lot* and didn't have much energy or strength for that matter.

On the day my dad was diagnosed, that evening we were still trying to come to terms with his diagnosis. We sat in his living room, having just finished dinner. Dad stared off into the distance. He sighed, then looked at me, and said, "This is going to be fast. I don't think I'll be here for Carleigh's graduation." The day he made that statement was March 25. The date for my daughter's graduation from high school was June 9.

Within around a month, my dad went from being an active, energetic, get-up-and-go person to someone who could not stay awake for more than an hour. He sat most of the day, and, when he managed to move around and try to do things around the house, he became winded and needed oxygen after only a 50-foot walk from his bedroom to the kitchen. A few times he bent down for something, lost all strength in his legs, and could not get back up.

He recently began having difficulty swallowing. He said it felt like his food "got stuck" in his throat. It took him a long time to eat anything, and he had to chew whatever he ate till his food was mush. He swallowed and drank lots of water after each bite. I could see the frustration, and I guess a little bit of fear, when he was trying to eat. These were the times when I felt helpless. I so wished there was something I could do for the man who had done everything for me. Lately, he'd been eating softer foods such as yogurt, ice cream, oatmeal, grits, and Ramen noodles. He also complained of being really hungry; when he thought of what he was going to eat, it sounded delicious, but when he started to eat, nothing tasted good and he lost his appetite.

"Why can't I get rid of this taste in my mouth?" he often complained. He had developed a terrible taste in his mouth and kept trying to figure out the cause. "Maybe it's that horrible cough medicine. Morphine? Maybe I'm not drinking enough water."

I listened but I had no suggestions to offer.

He also became shaky. This symptom came and went. At times he shook so badly that it was hard for him to hold his drink or his fork. He no longer wrote anything. When it was time to pay the bills, I wrote the checks and balanced his checkbook.

During those weeks after the diagnosis, some of his physical features changed. The one that stood out and surprised me the most was the swelling in his feet and ankles. My dad had the boniest feet and ankles. Now, his feet looked like pale stumps with toes sticking out from them. His feet, ankles, and up to his mid-calf displayed the same puffiness. He also had been bruising a lot. From what the hospice nurse told us, the morphine made him itch. He scratched and then bruised easily from it. He lost any muscle he had. The skin on his arms started to hang on him. His voice became hoarse, another symptom that came and went without any rhyme or reason.

Sometimes, things he said broke my heart and made it difficult for me to keep my composure around him. Frequently, when we were sitting in the living room, we'd make small talk while the TV played in the background. We'd stop talking for a moment and watch, and I would glance over at him and see that he was not paying attention to the TV. He gazed off into the distance and appeared lost in thought. There was a deep look of sadness and maybe fear on his face. He seemed to be a million miles away, and I could only imagine what thoughts were going through his mind. Seeing him so somber broke my heart.

Goober, my dad's beloved sidekick, is an adorable mutt with short, sandy brown hair. He's an older fella, and his muzzle has gotten mostly gray. Goober is not a big dog, not tall, and, well, okay, my dad feeds him a little too much. He stands about a foot high but weighs an easy 35 pounds. He goes wherever my dad goes.

One of those times when my dad and I were watching TV, I glanced to my left to look at Dad. The clear tubing from the oxygen snaked its way from the tank on the floor to his nose. His head was bowed forward slightly as he dozed. To his right, snuggled up right next to him, was Goober. My dad's right arm was draped along his back. Clearly, Dad fell asleep in mid-scratch. Goober's chin rested gently on my dad's lap. This was such a sweet sight that I just had to take a picture. Hopefully, sometime down the road, after time has passed, I can look at that photo and smile.

The other day, while we were standing out on my dad's front porch, my dad was enjoying his usual cup of coffee and cigarette (don't ask) while we talked. Goober was nearby, sunning himself in the tall, green grass of my dad's front yard. Dad casually motioned towards Goober and said, "I'm going to miss my little buddy when I'm gone."

That crushed me. Tears welled in my eyes. I felt so damn helpless so many times through this process. I sat, I asked, and I listened. Yet, I couldn't do a damn thing to really help him. Watching him slowly suffer and fade away was torture. I couldn't alleviate the pain or sadness he was feeling. That absolutely sucked; it was gut wrenching, frustrating, sad, frightening, angering, so many emotions! There were times I wanted to have the biggest pity party you've ever seen.

Nothing in life can prepare you for losing a loved one. We all realize that we will face these difficult moments in life, but we can't know how, when, or why until it happens. No one and nothing can get you ready or help ease the sadness, the feelings of helplessness and loss, but somehow we all go through it and survive.

I plan on doing more than surviving through this. My dad taught me to thrive. That's why I decided to journal during the time I had left with him. As much as it hurt, I would get through this. I would help him any way I could, and eventually, one day, the tears wouldn't flow as easily; the deep sense of loss wouldn't overwhelm me. The hurt and overwhelming sadness wouldn't stop me in my tracks. These things would be replaced with smiles, laughter, and gratitude for all my dad gave me.

Looking back, the first few weeks seemed relatively easy in comparison. That's the best way to describe them. By "easy" I mean that we had a schedule for him. Every three to four hours, he would take his morphine, nebulize himself, or as he liked to jokingly say, "gas himself." He would take his expectorant, use his oxygen as needed, and sleep occasionally. For the most part, he was slightly mobile and could walk through the house, make himself something to eat, and do his laundry. Of course, he got winded and tired more easily, but he felt productive when he did these little things. He slept well at night, getting a solid six hours, sleeping straight through.

Over time, Dad became a homebody. I tried to persuade him to get out, make a trip to the food store or take a short drive in the country. He did not comply. I tried not to push, but he had always been one to get up and go, no schedule, no time frame. He always loved to meander the country roads. Of late, he was willing to go only as far as his mailbox at the curb.

After about four weeks of casually nagging him, he agreed to a short trip to the local Walmart. We loaded the oxygen tank and brought the handicap parking sticker, and we were on our way! He was able to walk from the car to the entrance, and we got him situated in one of those motorized scooters. With list in hand, we shopped for about 10 items, then checked out, walked back to the car, and headed home. The trip lasted for all of about 30 minutes, but he felt so good that he had accomplished something, and he took a good, long nap afterwards!

Fast forward to today, and he shared with me that he feels he'll soon be bedridden. How quickly things change.

There were so many "last times" I would like to give him. I wanted to take him to the coast to walk along the beach one last time. I wished we could cruise on Carnival, go fishing together again, or catch and eat crabs. If only we could take one last trip and go out west to visit Bryce Canyon, Mt. Zion, Arches National Park. One last drive through the country, one final visit with my cousin Claudia, one last sailing trip, one more time to watch *Quigley Down Under*—all these moments and countless more I wanted to share with him one last time.

Recently, my dad had developed an intensely productive cough. He said it felt like something was stuck in the back of his throat, and he made this gargling sound as he tried to cough it up. He kept coughing to work it up and out and finally coughed up whatever was down there. What came up was not a pretty sight. The sound of him struggling to dislodge whatever was stuck and what he coughed up were equally bad. This stuff that seemed to collect in the back of his throat caused him to feel like he was choking at night when he slept.

"This stuff builds up in the back of my throat," he said. "And while I'm sleeping, I'm not coughing, so when it gets too built up, I wake up with the feeling like I can't breathe and I'm choking, so I have to have a few good coughs and all this yuck comes up," he described.

Lately, when he made the smallest coughing sound at night, I woke up, stared at the dark ceiling in my room, and waited. I waited for the sound of him getting the *yuck* up and then settling back into bed. Nighttime was the worst for this kind of stuff.

Dad attributed the pain in his back to his years of back problems. However, the cancer had spread to his bones, and, as the pain worsened, we knew what was really causing it.

The hospice nurse was here this morning. According to her, what my dad was experiencing was the normal progression of things. She suggested that increasing his morphine dosage and frequency should alleviate his shortness of breath, pain, and feeling of choking.

Her words echoed in my mind: "the normal progression of things." The end of that progression was death. My dad was progressing towards death, and it sucked.

As my dad's health worsened, as he weakened, he still found something to be thankful for, something to take pleasure in. The other day, as we stood on his porch once again, a beautiful, deep crimson-red male cardinal landed on the lower branch of a pine tree in his front yard. Dad watched him and looked around at the beautiful day before us. He took a deep breath, smiled, and said, "What a beautiful day—blue skies, sunshine, no humidity, a slight breeze. The birds are singing. What a beautiful day."

Countless times in my life, without even knowing it, my dad made me realize that, no matter how bad things got, you could always find happiness in something, and there was always something to be thankful for.

One more thing became clear to me through this process. I realized the wretched, depressing part in the process of dying from a terminal illness was how we lose parts of ourselves, ever so slowly, bit by bit, piece by piece. I guess that's why death is almost welcomed at some point. My dad was still able to find joy in small things, things most of us see every day yet take for granted. However, he was losing himself. He was slowly losing the ability to do the things that made Richard, Richard and the things he that brought him joy.

Every morning without fail at least for the 50 years I have known him, upon waking, my dad reached for his first cup of coffee and cigarette. He headed outside to take that first sip, that first drag. This he relished. As small or maybe gross or not understood by those of us who don't smoke, he found enjoyment in this morning ritual. He hasn't had a cup of coffee in about three days now. He regularly drank at least 12 cups of coffee in a day. He said he's lost his taste, his desire, for coffee.

As this disease progressed, he lost much of his independence. I started clipping his finger and toenails. My daughter began cutting his hair and helping him shave. I knew he was grateful for our help, but he was also frustrated that he could no longer do these little things for himself, and he had to rely on someone else to do them. These personal care routines most of us take for granted or even find annoying, but doing them himself meant he had some measure of independence.

Another loss had been walking his dog Goober. They used to take two daily walks without fail, one in the morning and another in the evening. They would stroll casually around the block, stopping to greet neighbors, talk, and catch up with the goings-on in their lives. It kept everyone connected, social, and involved. I took over the walking details. On most days I could only walk Goober once since I was still working. My dad missed getting outside, being active, visiting with his friends.

For us ladies, well, most of us, shoes bring great enjoyment—from the shopping to the outfit planning to the wearing. My dad, however, was a man of simple means. He had this pair of favorite sneakers from Roses, a small, discount store my dad frequented, and he loved to brag about his savings shopping there. His feet and ankles had become too swollen for him to wear those beloved sneakers anymore or shoes of any kind.

Another bit of joy lost to this disease was his love of a good Western starring John Wayne, Jimmy Stewart, or Clint Walker. His favorite station, Grit TV, showed Westerns 24/7. Those movies were not my cup of tea, but anytime I dropped by my dad's, Grit TV was on and he was watching. He had to start taking so much morphine that he couldn't stay awake for more than an hour or so. When he sat down to watch a Western, he dozed off almost immediately.

Many of us are well aware of the feeling when sleep eludes us and know how frustrating that can be. As his illness progressed, my dad got to the point where he had great difficulty sleeping through the night. Even though he was pretty heavily doped up on morphine, the choking cut into his slumber. Even though he slept elevated, fluid and food built up in the back of his throat, and he woke to the feeling of choking. He couldn't breathe in or out and ended up having to hack up that stuff that collected in the back of his throat. Once he cleared it, he had to sit up for a while and ended up having to cough up more. So, his sleep was broken, and, when he managed to sleep, he was suddenly awakened by the frightening feeling of choking.

The week of May 22, 2018, was not a good week for my dad. Just seven days earlier, he ventured out to Walmart. No big deal for most, but it was a huge accomplishment for him. As I reflected over those past days, I was amazed at how much his health had suddenly declined.

Within seven days, my dad had lost so much. Only a week earlier, he still enjoyed several cups of coffee a day, had two or three small meals, and walked throughout the house with relative ease. Yes, he would be winded and have to rest, but he walked with ease even though it was at a slower pace. He would occasionally venture out to the mailbox at the end of the driveway. He slept somewhat regularly. He engaged in our conversations.

On his third day without any coffee, he ate only two small yogurts, an egg over easy, a half a slice of toast, three strawberries, and a few sips of a banana and strawberry smoothie. He was experiencing so much back and hip pain that he could barely walk. When he tried, it was at a much slower pace with small, shuffling steps since he could no longer lift his feet. He slept close to 21 hours a day. Instead of the bed, he slept in his recliner in the living room, which helped to keep him elevated and alleviated his feeling of choking.

My dad could no longer be left alone. Up to this point, I went to the office early in the morning to work a half day, returned to my dad's place around 12:30, and worked the rest of the day there. Around 4:00 or so, I headed to my house, which was a mere five minutes away, to visit and spend some time with my kids. At home, I hung out with my kids for a bit as we talked about our day. They always asked how papa was doing. I showered, packed my clothes for the next day, and headed back to my dad's house.

On May 23, I woke up around 2:00 in the morning because I heard Dad moving around. He occasionally awakened in the middle of the night and went out to the porch for a cigarette. I heard him shuffle down the hallway. He poured himself a cup of coffee; I know this because the stainless-steel coffee pot made a distinct sound when it was placed on the countertop. I heard him put his cup in the microwave to heat his coffee. He unlocked the front door and went outside. I fell back to sleep.

I opened my eyes at 7:23 that morning. He was already up and out on the porch. I went outside; Goober followed me and made his way down the brick steps to perform his morning ritual of going to pee. I asked my dad, "How long did you stay up last night?"

He looked at me weird and said, "What?"

"How late did you stay up last night?" I asked again.

"What do you mean? I slept till 7:00 or so."

"I heard you get up around 2:30 last night, Dad."

He stared at me for a moment and said, "I did? No, I didn't."

I smiled, "Yes, you did."

He stared straight ahead and laughed. "Well, how about that. I have no recollection of getting up."

A look of worry on his face, I knew what he was thinking.

We came inside, and I went into the kitchen to get myself a cup of coffee. Apparently, not much of the coffee my dad poured for himself the night before actually made it into his cup. Dried coffee stains were all over the counter and on the floor.

What really made me nervous was the fact that my dad unlocked the door in his *unconscious* state. I knew then he couldn't be left alone while I was out. For the immediate future, my son would need to stay with him in the morning when I went to work, and one of my kids would have to be with him when I went to my house in the afternoon. Times were changing.

The pain my dad was experiencing that day was the worst it had been so far. He had pain in his lower back for years—years of not using proper form, of playing rough and tough as a boy and a young man. The middle-aged pot belly also added to the pain in his back. But this pain was different. This pain was from the cancer. It started in his lower back, in his spine particularly, but now had moved to his left hip. The pain was so excruciating he could barely walk. It was heartbreaking for me to watch him try to walk, stand, and sit. He held his hip and winced with every step. Even with the amount of morphine he was taking in combination with Advil, nothing made a dent in his level of agony. Times like these, I felt useless.

His movements were slow. Every move he made appeared arduous. He walked slowly, talked slowly, and moved his hands and arms in a measured way. He ate slowly. He turned his head, made facial expressions, glances, and eye contact deliberately.

Today, a new symptom began. Sometimes when he talked, he didn't make much sense. And he slept all…the…time. He would awaken to the slightest sound and respond with no coherence. He woke up just a little bit ago, and I asked him if he was hungry.

He responded, "No, that piece of steak filled me up."

I told him he hadn't had anything to eat today.

His eyes popped open. Looking puzzled, he asked, "I didn't just have steak?"

"No, Dad. Not today."

He stared for a moment, then his eyes drowsily closed, and he was asleep once again.

I had come to realize that the excessive sleep and lack of coherence was not because of the morphine. The hospice nurse said, "His body is preparing for death." Those were the worst words I'd ever heard in my life.

Early in this process, we had some really good conversations. He was the same old dad I've always known. He would debate, give his opinion, and start a conversation. We would sit and talk for a long time. This changed dramatically and was difficult for me to watch and accept. He was slowly shifting. He was no longer the same dad I remembered. He had grown quiet. He didn't start conversations anymore. When we talked, he only managed a single word comment. I'm already missing those opinionated statements that at one time frustrated me.

On Monday, May 28, 2018, the tides turned. My dad experienced some of the worst pain yet. He continued to sleep a lot. I followed my normal routine of going home around 4:00. My daughter, Carleigh, came to stay with him while he slept. I returned to my dad's house around 6:00 or so.

As I walked through the front door, he started to make his way from his office at the end of the hallway, the last room on the left. He stood in the hallway, frozen in his steps, and said, "I can't move."

I hurried back to him. He visibly winced in pain, something I have rarely, if ever, seen my dad do. I put my arm around him and asked, "Can I help you to the bed?"

He was holding on to the wall on each side of the hallway. He shook his head, still grimacing from the pain. My daughter came over and suggested that we take the rolling chair from his office.

"Good idea!" he confirmed.

She wheeled the chair behind him, and we gently eased him into it. The entire time his face was frozen with the pain he was feeling, and he let out a small groan.

He asked us to wheel him into the living room. But the pain was too intense for him to be able to move onto the couch. My worry for him deepened. We needed to get his pain under control and move him to his bed. It was time to call hospice.

The hospice nurse arrived around 7:30 that evening. I am ashamed to say I forgot her name, but she was absolutely amazing! Her demeanor and professionalism were top-notch.

Her compassion and the time she spent explaining everything, comforting, and reassuring all of us were beyond measure. I realized that his health had been slowly deteriorating since his diagnosis, but this day sealed the deal so to speak.

The nurse helped my dad make it to his bedroom, administered pain and anxiety medicines, put him in adult underwear, situated him comfortably in his bed, put his oxygen on, and covered him with his bed sheets. He immediately fell asleep. After she reviewed with us all the details to the changes of his medicines, the doses, frequency, the meds we needed to add to his cocktail, she took one last peak at my dad to make sure he was sleeping comfortably.

Then she sat with us in the living room. She told us something she probably had said a hundred times before: my dad was in the final stages of dying.

She gave my son and me a big hug goodbye, told us to call hospice for anything. "Don't hesitate," she said. She gathered her laptop and medical supplies and she left.

This first night was the longest. It was emotionally and physically draining. My dad slept solidly until 1:00 in the morning. I was sleeping in the room right across the hall from his. I could lean over in my bed and see him in his. I thought I heard him rustling, so I sat up and took a peek into his room. There he was, sitting up on the side of the bed.

"Dad, what do you need?" I asked him as I walked sleepily into his room.

He sat there with a blank, distant stare and said, "I need to pee."

"Dad, you can't walk into the bathroom; remember how bad your hip hurts."

I gently reminded him that he was wearing underwear that he could go to the bathroom in and told him that Bryce and I would help him change them. By now, Bryce walked sleepily into my dad's room.

"Papa, can I help you?"

There my dad sat, on the edge of the bed, staring. After a few quiet minutes, we asked him again, and he insisted he needed to get up, go to the bathroom, and pee.

He was confused, not making much sense. He reached over to the nightstand next to his bed and kept grabbing at the air.

"What do you need, Dad?"

"My thing." That was all he said. He finally grabbed onto the small flashlight on the nightstand, proceeded to draw it up to his lips and breathe in. I understood then. He was looking for his nebulizer. It had a mouthpiece where he breathed in the mist that contained the medicine. I gently held out my hand and he dropped the flashlight into my palm.

He stared for a moment and then said, "Your mom keeps waking me up, trying to give me medicine."

Of course, that was me. I was given orders by the hospice nurse that he was to have his morphine every two hours.

"Let's get you back into bed, Papa," my son suggested.

This banter between the three of us went on for about an hour. My dad would intermittently try to stand and walk towards the bathroom. Bryce and I would take hold of each arm and support him as we tried to convince him to sit down. He would forcefully demand that he "had to go pee." After several efforts and a lot of patience, we convinced him to lie back down. We got him comfortable, put on his oxygen, and gave him more medicine. Just as he began to get settled and started to fall asleep, he would fight sleep and sit up and again demand that he "had to go pee."

That began the course of events that continued for the rest of the night. Needless to say, neither one of us slept a wink. Through all of this, there was one moment when something my dad said struck me.

"Your mom is waiting for me. It's time to go home, Cyn."

This made me smile and gave me comfort knowing that my mom and all our loved ones who had gone before my dad were on the other side waiting to welcome him.

Towards the early hours of the morning, he began getting agitated and upset with us. At one point he demanded that we "get our Goddamn hands off of him." When we would suggest that we all go back to bed, his response was gruff: "Will you give it a break already?"

There were a few "funny" moments or at least moments that made us smile in the midst of all that was going on. I walked into the room and said, "Dad," and he responded loudly, "Cyn" (something he always calls me). For that brief moment, he sounded just like the old dad, my dad I'd known all my life.

A sudden wave of sadness washed over me. Reality hit me in the face once again. The man that was *my dad* was gone, and we were running out of time with what was left of him.

During one of his moments of demanding he had to pee, he stood up from sitting on the edge of the bed and pulled his private parts right out of the underwear and proceeded to try to pee. He did this more than once. Bryce frantically grabbed a bed pad that the hospice nurse had given us and tossed it on the floor at my dad's feet. Bryce and I giggled and smiled at each other. We weren't laughing at my dad but at how adamant and stubborn he was, even all drugged up and out of it and in his last hours of life here.

One of my greatest fears through this whole process was having to see my own father naked and clean him. Well, he ripped the Band-Aid right off that fear. Another moment, right after we put on a clean diaper (I hate using that word when referencing my father), he stood up and said, "Ta-da!" We couldn't help but smile at that. Even through his moments of being loopy, agitated, and angry at times, his sense of humor found its way out and made us smile.

Finally, around 5:30 in the morning, we couldn't take anymore. No matter how we tried, we could not get him to settle down and go to sleep. I made another call to hospice. Beatrice returned my call and suggested giving my dad another .5 ml of morphine with .5 mg of Lorazepam. About an hour later, another hospice nurse, Jenny, arrived. My dad finally settled down. Jenny took his vitals, increased his medicine, and got him situated and comfortable in bed.

On Tuesday, May 29, we had a rather quiet morning, thankfully. Heidi, our regular hospice nurse, came to check on my dad. Bryce, Heidi, and I all worked together to change him, his sheets, and get him clean and comfortable. She took his vitals; he now had a fever.

We all went to the kitchen to sit and talk. She showed me the pamphlet, "When Death Is Near." This is a manual of sorts for the signs that a caregiver of a terminally ill person can look for as they near the end of their journey. According to the signs, my dad was in the "days to hours" category. He was exhibiting seven out of the 11 signs for someone who is close to death. He was still in pain, so I relentlessly asked for something stronger than the morphine he was getting. Most of this was out of my control, but one thing I wanted to make sure of was that my dad was kept comfortable and out of pain for however long he had left.

All of this seemed so surreal. Two months earlier, if someone asked me what my greatest fear was, I would've said, without hesitation, "My kids dying before me and watching my dad slowly wither away and die." As I sat at my dad's kitchen table, he lay in bed down the hall, a mere 50 feet from me. At that moment, he was unresponsive, eyes closed, seemingly lifeless. His body was slowly shutting down, growing tired of working so hard to get a breath. He was dying. I was living out one of my worst fears. I sobbed.

I know there is no crystal ball to give us an insight to the timing of events as we move through our lives. There was so much going on in my life that I yearned, I begged the universe for a sign to show me how much longer my dad had to wait before he was called home to be with his Savior and his loved ones who passed before him.

My patience was nowhere to be found. Within the next three months, I needed to clean, pack, and put the house I had lived in and raised my kids in for the past 17 years on the market. My daughter would be leaving for college, and we needed to shop, pack, and schedule a few days to make the six-hour drive to Baltimore to the Maryland Institute College of Art and get her settled. That trip would offer a much-needed time away from everything I had been dealing with and living during those past few months. I looked forward to shopping for bedding, pillows, and decorations to make her room a home, to finding throw rugs, curtains, utensils, and gadgets for the kitchen, cleaning and shower supplies. I looked forward to moving her in, unpacking, setting up her room, and meeting her roommates.

Once all was said and done with my dad's journey here on earth, I had a multitude of financial paperwork to figure out and accounts to close. I faced moving and would have to decide what to do financially. I would tend to my dad's final wishes, tie up any lose ends, and figure out what to do with my dad's house and where to live myself. But during those final hours, we slowly cleaned up things at my dad's house as were his wishes. He started the process and asked that I continue once he could no longer perform those simple tasks. He wanted to make the cleanup process as he called it easier on me once he was gone. My daughter stayed at our home, helping me keep the house clean, vacuuming, washing dishes, and putting things in their place so when the time came the house would be ready to show to interested buyers. I hadn't done much in the way of packing up my house yet and still had closets, cabinets, and storage to go through.

Then there was work. I submitted the required documentation to take family medical leave. However, as supportive, kind, and patient my boss and my team had been, there were several loose ends I wanted to tie up before I took my leave. I planned to go into the office the next day for about an hour to make sure all was taken care of before I took time off for the next few weeks to tend to my personal affairs.

I became overwhelmed when I thought how all of this was happening at about the same time. But I had faith that God would see me through it. I couldn't wait to see what the other side of this journey would look like.

On Tuesday, May 29, we had a rough night. My dad's stubbornness still shone through. Even being heavily, and I mean *heavily*, medicated, he still fought sleep, rest, peace of any kind. We had him on a regular regimen of 1.5 milliliters of morphine every hour, 1 milligram of Lorazepam, and 1 milliliter of Haldol every four hours. This helped him to rest for an hour or so, but then he groggily awakened and tried to sit up. He always favored sleeping on his right side, so we propped him up on pillows so he could lean slightly to the right. He tried to prop himself on his right arm, but he was so weak that he trembled and wasn't able to move without some assistance. Bryce and I asked him what he needed or wanted, but he didn't respond. We asked him to lie down as we gently shifted him back to a reclining position. He stiffened when we moved him, resisting our efforts. No sooner than we got him to lie down again, he tried to sit up. This went on for a few minutes before he finally settled for maybe another hour or so.

His restlessness got to the point where neither Bryce nor I could settle him. Within another hour or two, Dad's breathing became extremely "wet." I was aware of the rattle dying people exhibited as they neared death, but this wet rattle sounded like he was going to choke, possibly suffocate, in his own fluids at any moment. I anxiously waited for the hospice nurse, who was stuck in traffic. Finally, at about 8:20 in the evening, Bob, the hospice nurse, arrived. After several milliliters of morphine, increasing his dosage of Lorazepam and Haldol, my dad finally settled down. Bob cleaned, situated, and readjusted him on his pillows, and we increased his oxygen to four milliliters to ease his breathing. We also used a small, wet sponge to clean my dad's mouth to help him absorb his medicine better.

Bob discussed the obvious with us. He told us that my dad was "exhibiting textbook end-of-life symptoms." As he explained it, as we near the end of our lives, our heart and lungs work extra hard to pump blood and breathe air. Once those muscles and organs are exhausted, we start to use our abdominal muscles to breathe. Anyone who has been with a loved one during this process knows what that type of breathing looks like. Because my dad's disease was in his lungs, these breathing issues were more pronounced in him.

For the rest of the night, Bryce and I worked on a rotation to give my dad morphine, Lorazepam, and Haldol every hour on the hour. My dad was unresponsive. He was finally resting after we did all that we could to make him comfortable. I couldn't help wondering if his slumber was caused by the heavy medications or if he was transitioning into the afterlife. My honest feeling was that my dad was halfway *home*, eternally speaking, and half here in this world. My dad was always a stubborn, hard-headed man, and that aspect of his personality was showing even in death. He was being stubborn and sticking around for some reason. I was not quite sure why.

When my turn in the rotation came to give him his medicine, I took the opportunity to talk to my dad. I climbed up on the bed next to him. There he lay, unresponsive, motionless, his mouth slightly open, his head tilted to the right. His big brown eyes, once full of brightness, life, and intention, were shut. I could detect no eye movement. I held his hand. He had strong, big hands. They were never perfectly clean. Because he was a man who always worked with his hands, they were weathered, and a little dirt still showed in the creases of his palm. The top of his hand was dotted with dark brown, oddly-shaped age spots. The arms that once swooped me up when I was little girl, that carried me up to bed, and hugged me with sweet, fatherly affection, were now just skin and bones.

I gently touched his forehead. My voice was shaky and emotional as I whispered, "Dad, I love you so much. Thank you for being the best dad anyone could ever have. You have taught me so much, given me so many wonderful memories and life lessons. Thank you for being the best Papa to my kids. I want you to know it's okay to go home and be with Mom, Grandma and Grandpa, Aunt Marie, and Uncle Jimmy. We all love you and we will take care of each other and everything here. There's no reason to hold on, Dad. You've done well. You deserve to be happy. You better promise me that you'll be there, waiting for me and helping me cross over when it's my time."

Tears easily flowed down my cheeks and fell onto my shirt, making small, round dots. I realized this was the last conversation I would have with my dad. I reluctantly placed his hand back under the covers, kissed his forehead, and whispered in his ear, "I love you, Dad." Just two days earlier, he was somewhat alert, responding to my questions. He knew I was there with him and felt my presence. He was now a body lying in his bed, his spirit… gone. My heart was literally breaking.

It was getting excruciating for me to watch my father in this state. His frail body, his sunken face, lifeless eyes. How could a man who was so full of life, personality, sarcasm, humor, be so motionless and lifeless? His breathing was painful to listen to and watch. His poor body worked so hard to get that breath in. His breath was becoming shorter, shallower, and slower. He took only about six breaths in a minute. The wet gargling sound of his breathing was something I could almost no longer bear to hear. When we give him his medicine, we swabbed his mouth. He was no longer swallowing. As his saliva collected in his mouth, it had a thick, yellow, foamy consistency. I carefully swabbed his mouth and lips with cool water, wiped his face with a cool, wet rag. As I administered his medicine, I always said, "I love you." I kept asking him why he was being so darn stubborn and holding on.

The next day, Wednesday, we had a quiet morning. Not much had changed. Bryce and I were exhausted. I prayed that this didn't last much longer. It was painful and heartbreaking to watch my dad lie there the way he was. We continued to give him meds every hour on the hour. Around 1:00 in the afternoon, Heidi, my dad's regular hospice nurse, stopped by to check on him. She decided to put on a fentanyl patch. She said that once the fentanyl patch took effect, in about 12 to 18 hours, we could reduce the number of times we gave him morphine, allowing us to get some rest. Before she left, she gave each of us a big hug.

My son, Bryce, was incredible during this journey. From the moment my dad was diagnosed, he handled things at home for me. He cleaning up after himself and around the house. Knowing I was stressed about cleaning up the yard to get our house ready to sell, he cleared around the outside of the house as well. One day I went home to find that he had power washed the front porch, the deck, and the patio in back. He was in the process of getting rid of the weeds in the backyard, making it look nice.

At times when I couldn't bear to see my father struggling or to face having to clean him, my son took control with the hospice nurse. He helped hospice with moving my dad and changing his sheets. He never once hesitated to take my turn when it came to giving my dad his meds. On more than one occasion, he would say, "Mom, I've got this; it's okay."

He would comfort me when he saw me breaking down. I could not have gotten through those days and months without him. I am beyond proud of the young man he has become.

In the midst of my pain, my worries, my lack of sleep, questions, and uncertainty, hospice also was an absolute godsend. In those last few days, I spoke to and met a dozen different nurses and people who worked with the Wake County Hospice. *Every single person was absolutely amazing!* Everyone was first and foremost professional as well as personable, friendly, caring, empathetic, knowledgeable, and confident in their care of my father. They met our needs and then exceeded them. They gave us incredible care and comfort beyond measure. I would not have been able to do what I needed to do without their constant help and support. I will be forever grateful for each and every one of them.

On Wednesday, May 30, 2018, Carleigh stopped by around 9:00 in the evening. She was there for a brief moment the previous day but hesitated going into my dad's room. She was struggling with seeing him in this state. We discussed this, and she shared she was feeling a little guilty. I told her to pray about it but not to feel bad. This was a personal thing, and there was no right or wrong.

After she arrived, she came into my room and sat on the bed. She glanced across the hall at her papa lying in bed. At 9:15 that night, I gave him his rounds of medicine. I talked to him as I usually did, but this time I also discussed the reassurance I felt because he had been able to meet and approve of my fiancé, Will. My dad had gotten to know him and had seen the good man that he is. He had told me just a few weeks earlier that he was happy I had met a good man and that I would not be alone.

"I love you, Dad," I said again. "Stop being so stubborn. We all love you and want you to be at peace. Please go be with Mom. I'm so thankful that you and Will got to know each other and that you approve of our relationship. We will take care of each other. Your grandkids are in a good place. They are incredible young adults. Thank you for helping me raise them."

I kissed him on the forehead as I did every time before and whispered in his ear, "I love you, Dad."

I looked over my shoulder and realized Carleigh had come into Dad's bedroom. I guessed she had heard some of what I said to him. Her eyes welled with tears. She walked over to the side of the bed and caressed her papa's arm.

"Hi, Papa," she said crying. I asked her if she wanted to be alone with her papa, and she gave a simple nod.

I left the room, crying at the beautiful moment that she and her papa would share. I sat in my room and wept. I couldn't hear what she was saying to her papa, but I could hear her sobbing. She returned to my room about 15 minutes later. Without saying a word, I could tell that she was glad she got to spend some time with her papa.

"I told him I loved him. I told him he should go and be with Nana. I said my goodbyes to him."

She wasn't upset as she spoke; she was calm, composed, and there was a sense of peace within her. We casually talked for a few minutes about her upcoming graduation from high school, her boyfriend, and end-of-year projects she needed to finish.

I stopped and listened. "I don't hear Papa breathing," I said. I got up and walked into his room.

"Dad?" I said. Walking closer to him, I looked for the raising of his abdominal area and listened for the gasping for breath.

"Dad?" I said again. I felt his chest. I couldn't find his heartbeat. I watched his chest for any sign of breathing. Nothing. I glanced over at Carleigh and shook my head.

"Is...he...gone?" she asked.

"I think so, baby."

"Papa?" She sat on the bed next to him and stroked his arm, felt his head. "Papa?" She felt his chest. "He's not breathing," she said.

He was gone. I touched his forehead; he was cool. I felt his chest: no faint heartbeat. I looked over at my daughter, sitting next to her papa, and I cried.

"My dad's gone." I held his hand and told him for the last time that I loved him, that I was happy he was no longer suffering and he was now with Mom. In that surreal moment, the idea hit me that the one person that had meant the most to me, that had made the biggest impact on my life, whom I had known longer than anyone...was no longer here.

Carleigh called her brother and let him know that Papa had died. (Earlier in the day, he asked if he could go to dinner with his friends and said he would be back within the hour.) I told him to go, thinking there wouldn't be much of a change, at least for the next few hours.

Bryce walked through the front door 10 minutes later. He walked over to me and said, "Mom." I took a few steps towards him, and he gave me the tightest hug he had ever given me, and I broke down in his arms. He held me tightly as I sobbed.

He whispered, "He's not suffering anymore."

I wept and thanked my son. I thanked him for stepping up and showing me the incredible, caring, compassionate yet strong young man he had become. This young man helped me in ways I could not begin to describe. As I thought about all he had done for me and his papa during those final days, I beamed with pride, so thankful to be his mom.

I watched as my son walked down the hall towards his sister. My kids at times weren't exactly the best of friends. They had a difficult relationship. Bryce walked over to his little sister and hugged her tightly. I watched, tears flowing, with a mixture of sadness and pride as my two babies, now young adults, hugged each other in love, sadness, and understanding that their papa was gone.

I started to call hospice, and as I thought, "What do I say?" I guess I said it aloud. I knew what to tell them; it just felt weird to say the words: "My dad has died." It just didn't sound or feel right.

Bryce took the phone from my hands, saying, "Mom, let me do this."

I cannot express the overwhelming feeling of pride I truly have for my son. My cup runneth over.

There was a knock on the door about 10 minutes later. Time stood still during those minutes as we waited for hospice.

There my dad lay in his bed, motionless. His chest no longer heaved in pain, gasping for breath. His body no longer had to fight so hard to force that breath in. I could see already that the pink hue his skin held just a few moments earlier was now already turning a dull, sullen gray. His face was frozen in the state it was for the past two days: head slightly tilted to the right, his mouth gaping open. Over the last 24 hours or so, his jaw had become rigid.

I felt a bit of relief hearing that knock at the door.

"Hi. I'm from hospice." She said her name, and, in that moment overwhelmed by all my emotions, I didn't even hear some of what she was telling me. Softly, she said to us, "I'm so sorry for your loss."

"Thank you," Bryce said, and we motioned her to the back of the house to my dad's bedroom.

We stayed out of my dad's room as the hospice nurse examined him and confirmed his death. She emerged from his room a few minutes later.

"I'm so sorry. Yes, he is gone."

She stated a simple fact we already knew was true.

"What would you like him to be dressed in?" she asked.

Hmm. This was something I didn't even think about. My dad's wishes were to be cremated with no memorial service. He always said, "Celebrate me while I'm alive, and don't worry about me when I'm gone."

I looked at Bryce and Carleigh, and I could tell we had the same thought.

"Jeez, I never thought about what to dress him in," I announced as I walked to his closet. We stood there, staring at his clothes, and the decision was easy. My dad basically wore four things: jeans or shorts, short-sleeved T-shirts with a pocket, or long-sleeved flannel shirts. It took us only a few moments. We picked out a black-and-red checked flannel shirt, a pair of jeans, underwear, and socks. We also wanted to send him off with a pack of Winston Reds 100 and a Marine hat. I hope my dad was happy with the choices we made.

The nurse kindly asked us to excuse ourselves so she could dress my dad for the last time. She closed the door behind us, emerging about 10 minutes later. Once that was done, we all went to the living room and sat down. She opened her laptop, entering the information that would be on my dad's death certificate. (Remembering that gives me chills.) She told us he was all dressed if we wanted to see him.

Carleigh asked if she could go home, and I said, "Of course." I could tell she wasn't comfortable with seeing the funeral home come and take her papa away.

"I love you, Mom," she said.

"I love you, baby," I replied. I gave my sweet girl a hug and a kiss and sent her on her way.

A few minutes later, someone from Thomas Funeral Home arrived. A very tall, dark-haired young man walked in. He was dressed casually in pants and a short sleeved shirt. It was, after all, late in the evening, and May in North Carolina was hot.

"I'm so sorry for your loss," he said offering his condolences.

"Thank you."

He asked us a few questions regarding my dad's wishes. I told him he wanted to be cremated with no service. He asked us to give him a few minutes to get my dad, and we could say our last goodbyes to him. Both Bryce and I told him we already said our farewells.

We also informed the young man that we didn't want to see my dad wheeled out on the stretcher, covered with a dark, plastic sheet. We waited in the kitchen while they put my dad on the stretcher.

When they were ready to wheel his body out, down the hallway and out the door, Bryce said, "Mom, call Goober. He'll get underfoot. Kneel down and talk to him and pet him to keep him by you."

Goober came running over to me, and, as I knelt down to converse with my dad's sidekick, I realized exactly what my son was doing. You see, where I was standing in the kitchen, I would still be able to see them wheeling my dad past us. But, kneeling down, they would be out of my sight.

I smiled to myself. "I know exactly what you're doing, and thank you," I said to my son.

He gave a slight shrug and smiled.

Chapter 7: Time for Mourning

It was all over. These past two months, everything I feared, stressed over, tried to coordinate, figure out, and handle were over. It had been two months of living with my dad, working, and going home every day to visit my kids. All of it had ended: the cleaning and errands for my dad, the special moments of sitting and talking with him about everything, the moments of sadness and fear, the hospice visits, the cards of encouragement sent from friends, the time of watching his health decline, the routine and rounds of medicine, all the praying and crying.

At 11:36 p.m. on Wednesday, May 30, hospice, the funeral home, and my dad were gone. It was just Bryce and me. Bryce walked over to the kitchen cabinet that housed the few bottles of liquor my dad had. My dad rarely drank, but when he did his favorite drink was Sambuca. Bryce reached for the clear bottle with the silver and blue label. It was still half full. I think my dad had that bottle for about 10 years.

Bryce grabbed two plastic cups and poured us each a shot. Without saying a word, we went outside to the porch, Goober following along. Bryce pulled out a Winston Reds 100 cigarette and lit it. He handed it to me, and I took a drag. He raised his glass of Sambuca, I raised mine, and we cheered, "Here's to Papa."

We each took a sip of the Sambuca. The strong alcohol content and the fact that I rarely drank made me cough. The liquid warmed and burned my throat and chest as it made its way down. There we stood in the light of the full moon and the warmth of a North Carolina late spring night. It was quiet except for the crickets chirping. Lightning bug flashes sparked in the background. Goober lay on the porch beside us.

Without saying a word, it felt natural to go to my dad's room.

"I thought I saw something in Papa's drawer when you opened it up to get him a pair of socks," Bryce said.

He opened that drawer and there was a black box. In it, we found cufflinks, a few rings, my dad's wedding band, some older pictures of me that were obviously weathered and faded that he must have kept in his wallet at some point. We also found a .32 caliber handgun, unloaded. Bryce smiled seeing that .32. He picked it up, admiring it. He checked the chamber. There were loose bullets in the drawer.

My dad was an admirer and highly knowledgeable lover of history and guns. We both laughed because earlier Bryce had said, "You know we're probably going to find more guns in the house." Earlier that day, we were admiring the 15 guns my dad kept in the gun safe in the third bedroom closet. There were also some other trinkets. The more we went through things, we realized that my dad kept *everything,* and he kept it everywhere.

We found some family pictures. Then Bryce noticed a silver lock box that wasn't locked. Opening it, we discovered a picture of my grandfather, my dad's dad. As far as I knew, there was only one picture of my great-grandmother, Grandma Frederikka Wedel. She was my dad's grandmother on his mom's side. She was Bryce's great-great grandmother. It's a typical black-and-white picture from that time period. Simple. She was standing, hands at her side. Her gray hair was pulled back into a bun and she wore glasses. Her face was expressionless, not smiling, not frowning. She didn't look mean; she appeared demure. She was wearing a flower-patterned dress which came to mid-calf. Her shoes were a not-so-attractive, manly-looking style in a basic black.

I finally started to feel drowsy. "It's 12:30," I said. "We should get some sleep."

Bryce agreed and we closed my dad's bedroom door behind us as we left the room. As I lay in bed that first night without my dad across the hall, I cried. "I love you, Dad. I'm so thankful you didn't suffer and lay there for days. Thank you for everything you've done for me. Sleep well, Dad; sleep well."

I woke up around 7:30 the next morning. I had slept but not soundly. My mind was still overloaded with the memories and stress of the past few days and especially of the previous night. Goober hopped off the bed, giving a good stretch to get the sleep out of his bones. I opened my door and Goober ran right to my dad's bedroom door, tail wagging, looking over his shoulder at me, anxiously waiting for me to open the door so he could say good morning to my dad as he had done many, many times before.

I opened the door for him and he scooted right in, tail still wagging. He stopped and glanced at the bed, excitedly ran around to the other side of the bed, tail wagging, but now he looked back at me, confused, as if to ask, "Where is he?"

I cried and I cried hard. It was incredibly difficult for me to watch Goober excitedly expecting to greet my dad and realizing he wasn't there anymore. You could actually see the disappointment on Goober's face.

"I know, Goober; it's weird, isn't it? I miss him too." I knelt down beside my dad's beloved companion, stroked his soft, brown fur, and cried. I felt so incredibly sad for this sweet boy. My dad loved him dearly and expressed concern for his wellbeing after he was gone. I promised my dad we would take care of him and love him as much as he did.

I was quiet as I crept out of my bedroom and to the kitchen to make some coffee. Bryce was sleeping soundly on the couch in the living room. There was a stillness about this morning—the first day in 17 years that I had been in my dad's house without him there. It felt strange to use his coffee pot, his coffee cup, the milk in his refrigerator as if I were using his stuff without his permission. Of course, he never made me feel this way, but for some reason in that moment, I wanted his permission to be casually walking through his house in those rooms, using *his* things.

It was overcast that morning. The air was thick with typical late spring North Carolina humidity. The weather forecast called for storms all week long. For the most part, the days had been cloudy with thunderstorms occasionally rolling through. Fortunately, there were moments when the sun peaked through, shining on the leaves, the trees, and the ground below.

I spent the morning reaching out to those who were close to us, sharing the news of my dad's passing. I also needed to stop by the funeral home to make final arrangements.

The morning was overwhelming. I was inundated with an outpouring of love, sympathy, and support from so many people. Everyone from casual acquaintances to family and best friends reached out to me. I was beyond humbled by this show of human kindness and compassion. By 11:30 that morning, a beautiful plant had already arrived from my friends at work. As sad as this time was, I felt beyond blessed by those whom God had brought into my life.

That day was also somewhat of a blur. Along with accepting the many expressions of love and sympathy, Bryce and I started easing into the process of going through a few things. This may seem too soon or callous to some, but my dad kept telling me, even up to a few days before his death, to start cleaning and making his place my own if I wanted to. In the midst of his own impending death, he was concerned about making things as easy for me as possible after he was gone. We talked about what he wanted me to hold on to, his financial wishes for me, and the things he wanted his grandchildren to have, those items that held a great deal of sentimental value for him.

I needed to pack my own house and bring things to my dad's place. I had a lot of packing, moving, and unpacking to do in the next few months. My dad understood this, and he felt good knowing he was leaving me a place to live if I wanted it.

By 4:30 that afternoon, rain poured hard against the roof, and gusts of wind thrashed tree branches. It looked like a tropical storm outside as I pulled into the parking lot of Thomas Funeral Home. The building was a gorgeous white, three-story, century-old home. A beautiful wrap-around porch with thick circular, etched columns led to enormous double doors that opened into the foyer. The wood inside was dark brown with a shine to it. The molding and trim were eight inches high on the walls. The floors were carpeted. It had a slight musty odor but in a comforting way like the scent of grandma's house. You could smell the history in the home. I felt oddly comforted by this place.

I was led into Tim's office. He was an older gentleman with graying hair, a receding hairline, and a matching gray mustache. He wore glasses.

"It's nice to meet you, Ms. Beardslee. I'm sorry we are not meeting under different circumstances," he said.

"Thank you," I replied. We went through all the necessary paperwork required by law. He led me upstairs to the display of different urns they offered. I chose a dark cherry wooden urn for my dad. Tim suggested engraving the Marines emblem on the front, and I loved the idea.

When all was said and done, Tim informed me that my dad's ashes, the 10 copies of his death certificate I requested, and the flag for his years of service as a Marine would be ready for me to pick up the following Wednesday.

He shook my hand and said, "I want to say thank you for allowing me to take care of your father. I have a great deal of gratitude for our veterans. Thank you to your dad for serving our country."

I was touched by his sweet words and sentiment. "Thank you; I appreciate that." I smiled and left.

It's amazing how much a person can end up learning to do for the first time. My life had become of series of learning to do things I would never have believed I could before they happened.

That day was full of emotions and finality as I realized a chapter of my life had closed. If I thought too much about the huge amount that remained to be done, I began to feel overwhelmed, and the pressure and weight of it caused me great anxiety.

Bryce decided to sleep at our house for the night. Tonight was the first night I would be sleeping alone in my dad's house. I was not looking forward to it and actually dreaded it. I felt strange sleeping in his house by myself. It was too quiet, too still. I closed the door to my dad's room. For some reason I just couldn't sleep with his door open right across from the room where I slept. I didn't sleep soundly. I woke a few times, each time glancing at my dad's door.

Friday, June 1, was quiet. Bryce and I worked a little more on going through some of my dad's things. As I've said it before, my dad saved *everything!* We found car registrations from the 1990s, his life insurance information from a company he worked for that closed back in the early 1980s, and receipts from food stores for miscellaneous things from 10 to 12 years past! We unearthed a treasure trove of photos; my mom and dad took pictures of everything. A lot of them were in triplets. A lot of work lay ahead of us.

As we were going through things, I noticed a white envelope in the bottom drawer of my dad's dresser. I was careful grabbing it as it was open and had a few heavier items inside that might fall out. He had saved my Girl Scout and Brownie pins! He also had kept this corny little gift I made him when I couldn't have been older than eight or nine. It was half of a walnut shell, and, on the flat side, I had glued a cut out picture of me dressed in my ballerina costume for a dance recital. I discovered this tiny, three-by-three-inch piece of paper where I had written in colored markers, Cindy and Daddy. I had drawn two paint brushes with a paint palate and three little colorful flowers. I was probably six or seven when I made that for him. I had written the y's backwards. The drawing was folded in fourths. I cannot believe he saved that little piece of paper I gave him so long ago. Seeing this brought tears. Just another confirmation of his love for me as his *little girl.* Many things we were finding made me smile; a few made me cry. I was already missing my dad so much.

A couple of quieter days passed as the condolences, phone calls, and deliveries slowed down. I was thankful for that. Bryce and I started the process of cleaning rooms. We struggled with the idea of it being too soon but decided that Dad would be okay with us moving forward. I believed that in my heart. Early on, he made it perfectly clear that he wanted me to take the house when he was gone.

"Make this place your own," he had said. "Living here will give you a chance to catch your breath, save some money. Somewhere down the road, when you're ready to sell it, you'll make a nice penny for your retirement."

Up until the very end, he was always worried about me, his little girl. Have I mentioned that I'm so proud to be his daughter?

I finally got back to feeling like myself a little. I spent some much needed and missed quality time with Will. I met him for dinner on Saturday night, and we had some good conversations and catching up. The two of us were never at a loss for words; we are both chatterboxes. At times we competed to get a word in. We reminisced about my dad, and Will mentioned how grateful he was for getting to know my dad those last few weeks. He came to see that my dad really was the good man I had been bragging about.

On Sunday, Will and I walked the streets of downtown Raleigh and the NC State campus. It was a hot day, but there were some clouds and we enjoyed the beautiful breeze. We had a drink at a local restaurant, sitting at one of their rooftop tables.

Monday, June 4, 2018, was the first night I slept in my own bed in my own house in over two months. I fell asleep as soon as my head hit the pillow. I was awakened during the night to our tuxedo cat, Vader, purring and tapping his sweet, soft, warm paw against my arm. That was his way of asking me to let him under my blanket so he could snuggle close to me, something I definitely missed while I stayed with my dad.

I had so much to do at my house: cleaning, packing, donating, throwing things out, moving things to my dad's house. The cleaning was going to be a huge undertaking. I'm a neat freak by nature, so I wanted everything spotless and just right before I put the house on the market. The carpets needed to be cleaned.

The black dog hair from our two labs was collecting everywhere. When I clean, I tackle baseboards, walls, furniture, blinds—it all gets wiped down. I needed to declutter. I remembered from selling our first house that decluttering and putting away any personal photos were a necessity.

I looked around and didn't know where to begin. The upstairs bonus room, a large space, was completely full of bags and boxes to be donated. I needed to drop those off and clean out that room before I began going through more things to throw out or donate. I was feeling overwhelmed.

What did I really *want* to do? *Nothing*. I had been living in overdrive for a few months. At this point, nothing would have made me happier than to just sit outside on our deck and take in the beautiful weather, read a book, have a glass of wine, and enjoy our big, beautiful yard before I had to leave.

But it was time to run errands. I needed groceries, gas, and a stop at the bank. I also had to make some phone calls and pay some bills. When I got the copies of my dad's death certificate, I knew I would have a lot to do, all of which I'd never done before.

Today was a beautiful day. The sun was shining and it was a typical warm spring day in North Carolina. A slight breeze and almost no humidity made the temperature tolerable. I thought I just might take that break at some point in the day.

I've been blessed with wonderful friends throughout my entire life. Some came into my life for just a season; some I have known just about my entire life. It's been said that you know who your true friends are in the hard times. Take a look around and who's standing by your side, loving you, supporting you, helping you through the rough patches; those are the people you hold on to and never let go.

When I think of my closest and dearest friends, I recall several happy, funny memories with them. Within those happy memories, there were some difficult, sadder times as well. During those sad, trying times, whether they were my own or one of my dear friends, we all came together to support and love each other, to do whatever we could to help.

The outpouring of love and support that my friends, acquaintances, my dad's friends, even my coworkers showed after my dad's passing was overwhelming. When my dad was first diagnosed and during the following weeks while I was living with him, my closest girlfriends often sent me a quick text, checking in on me, seeing if I needed anything, letting me know they were praying for us. My dearest friend, Arrie, who lives 600 miles away, was always checking up on us and praying for us. After my dad died, she planned to visit me, and the time of her arrival was only a few days away. She wanted to help me get my house ready to sell. Arrie was always there for me, always.

My coworkers and my entire department were patient and supportive. My boss allowed me to take a day off here and there whenever I needed it. My coworkers picked up the slack for me at work when I couldn't be there. Each of them expressed their love, prayers, and support.

My dad was an intensely private man during all of this and, when he was diagnosed, he didn't want everyone to know. There were two couples who lived in his neighborhood with whom he chose to share this deeply personal news. One of those was John and Elaine. John was a Marine like my dad; they happened to be stationed at Parris Island at the same time, but they never met back then. Fast forward 50 plus years, and they lived one block away from each other. Small world.

My dad spoke highly of John. I knew all about him, his time spent as a Marine, his two dogs, a beautiful older shepherd,

Kia, with long, dark fur and the typical long, pointed ears that shepherds have. She was an older, gentle soul. Then there was Dexter, a beautiful white and black pitbull puppy. Although he was actually over a year old, his puppy came out whenever John walked him. All he wanted to do was visit everyone and give kisses. A massive dog with large features, his kisses alone could knock over a grown person, but he was such a love. When John walked him, he was also training him, although Dexter would rather have been socializing.

The other couple my dad shared the news with was Norma and Willie. I truly believe Norma was brought into my dad's life, especially mine, for a reason. There are no coincidences. Norma became a close, trusted friend to me, almost a mother figure. I had the wonderful opportunity to have some heartfelt conversations with Norma, and we shared a lot, realizing we had much in common.

Every morning, without fail, Norma walked her adorable dog, Zoey, a hyper, excitable, sweet, little black dog with delicate features and a bark and whine to match. She and Goober became friends, an item of sorts, and they could hear the other one outside and always wanted to play together.

I met Norma one morning while she was walking Zoey. By Zoey's excitement, it was apparent that they would stop and visit with my dad every morning. That particular day was no different. My dad was on his porch, performing the ritual of his morning cup of coffee and cigarette. I decided to enjoy my cup of coffee on the porch with him. As Norma and Zoey were making their way down the sidewalk, Zoey spotted my dad and Goober and started yanking, pulling, barking and yelping, tail feverishly wagging. Pulling Norma, she excitedly ran up my dad's driveway. While Goober and Zoey played, rolling around, smelling, and chasing each other, Norma introduced herself.

She was this sweet, genuine, do-for-others lady. From the moment we met, we clicked. I felt an overwhelming sense of faith, peace, and comfort with her. She sent me a devotion every morning without fail. She wished us a good day and asked God to bless us.

On more than one occasion, Norma's husband Willie took my dad to his eye doctor appointments. They would visit and talk. Both Willie and Norma were good friends to my dad and became special to me as well. Norma was always worrying about my dad, bringing him smoothies to make sure he was eating, extra pillows to help raise him during sleep when his breathing became bad, and cards with words of prayer and encouragement. She would stop by and offer to walk Goober on days when we couldn't. They both were a godsend and I pray that God blesses them abundantly.

My friends volunteered to help us pack and move. Donna made us a delicious chocolate cake (per my son's request). My supervisor and coworkers chipped in and had dinner delivered to us. Diane offered to do laundry and cook dinner. The list of love and support from my friends went on and on; I am blessed by some beautiful people in my life.

There was a soft knock on my front door around 8:30 in the morning on Tuesday, June 10. The dogs barked and ran to the front door and immediately started whining with excitement. There, at my front door, stood a petite woman with long auburn hair, wearing black yoga pants and a graphic tee. She had a huge smile on her face. One of my dearest and closest friends, Pam, had come to visit me.

She gave me the tightest embrace and didn't let go. "How are you?" she whispered in my ear.

We pulled back from our hug and I looked at her. "I'm good. I've had my moments, but I'm very thankful for the two months I had with him."

I made us a pot of coffee, and we spent the next four hours catching up. We hadn't seen each other in months, and so much had happened in both our lives.

When my kids came home, they gave her big hugs. Both of them adored Pam and had known her since they were little. My kids filled her in on what was going on in their lives.

I decided to take Pam to my dad's house. She had never seen it, and I wanted to get her opinion on a few things and to introduce her to Goober. Goober, of course, loved Pam. There isn't a human Goober doesn't love. I walked Pam through the rooms, which were disorganized and cluttered at this point as we tried to figure out what to keep. We had been cleaning, painting, and packing, so everything was in disarray.

The day was beautiful, so we decided to take Goober for a walk. His walks were always around the one block my dad's house was on, usually taking no more than 10 or 15 minutes, depending on how casual Goober's gait was. We walked and talked. Pam looked at the quaint, one-story houses on the street and liked what she saw.

"I feel happy here. This street is adorable. The houses are all so pretty. I wish I could live here."

Although I didn't get any cleaning or packing done on the day Pam arrived, spending time with her, talking and sharing, did me and my heart a world of good. I felt profoundly blessed.

Since I was 15, I'd always started my day with a cup of coffee, something I got from my dad. The next morning, as I sat on my bed sipping my hot cup of coffee, my two black labs, Ryder and Braxton, were lying next to me. Braxton was dreaming, whimpering, barking a sleepy, muffled bark, his feet twitching. Ryder was beside me curled up in her tight, little ball; this was how she always slept.

The pressure of getting things done was starting to stress me. Three hours later, I began the arduous task of cleaning, packing away personal pictures, going through more things I could donate. The next step was to go to my dad's house and do laundry and clean some more.

I was putting away one of the several bags of things I had brought over to Dad's house when I found two pictures of my dad. One was of him standing on the docks at the coast. He was dressed in typical Richard fashion: a hat, flannel shirt, jeans, and sneakers. It was hard to tell, but it looked like he was holding a cigarette in his right hand. The other photo was a close-up of his profile. He had his glasses on and was wearing a white, short-sleeved T-shirt. His arms were casually folded on the table where he sat, and a pack of cigarettes lay in front of him. This picture made me cry. It was a casual picture of him, but seeing a close-up of the face I'd known for 50 years, looking healthy, happy, in the moment, made me miss him terribly. I still couldn't believe he was gone.

While I was driving to my dad's house, I got a phone call from the funeral home. They said my dad's death certificates were ready to pick up. All of this seemed surreal. I went to his home, and he wasn't there. His coffee cup, the one he constantly drank coffee from, sat on the countertop, and it hadn't been used in almost two weeks. A pack of Winston filtered cigarettes, half empty, sat on his nightstand, his lighter right next to it. His comb, Barbasol shaving cream, razor, Speed Stick deodorant, lay on his bathroom vanity in the exact spot where he placed them the last time he used them. The slippers he always wore were on the floor beside his bed as he left them the last time he took them off. They were misshapen in the mold of his feet. The heels and once furry insides were flattened and worn with impressions of his soles, mirroring his narrow feet. I hadn't heard his voice for a week, something that had never happened in my 50 years of having him in my life.

My dad had this heavy winter sweater he would wear to go outside and smoke a cigarette with his coffee. It hung on the back of the door leading to the garage. It hadn't been touched since the last time he draped it there about a month earlier. As long as I could remember, he had that sweater. I have pictures of him wearing it from 15 to 20 years earlier. It was a dark blue and white, small-stitched sweater with dark blue knitted trim around the waist, wrists, and neckline. It zipped up the front and had two pockets. After so many years, the white had turned a dingy gray color, and there were some tears in the knitting. One pocket was ripped, and it smelled of cigarettes. I walked over to it and took it off its hanger. I held it in my hands then hugged it close to me. I buried my face in that sweater and took a long, slow, deep breath. I cried.

My dad's bedroom was jam-packed with things we needed to sort through. The sheets that he lay in those last few days were still on the bed. His clothes were exactly where he left them. It all still smelled of his illness, and I found it difficult to be in that room. The sadness overwhelmed me when I went into his bedroom.

The next day, I was feeling lazy and unmotivated. I knew I had a lot to prepare before the realtor came on Monday, but, instead of actually doing anything, I sat there in bed. That Saturday would be Carleigh's graduation from high school. Family would be coming into town to celebrate with us. It was going to be a nice day with lots of family time, celebrating my daughter's achievements. However, there would be a touch of sadness as well because my dad wouldn't be there. He had predicted that he wouldn't make it to her graduation; he missed the occasion by only 10 days.

On Friday, June 8, 2018, as soon as I opened my eyes at 6:30, my head began throbbing with a horrible migraine. Recently, my migraines had been getting worse in intensity and length. Anyone who suffers from migraines can relate to the extreme pain they cause. Most times, when I felt a migraine coming on, I would take an Imitrex and, within an hour or so, I felt better. I experienced side effects of the medicine such as a sore throat, skin sensitivity to hot and cold, and a runny nose. The two migraines I had over the previous two weeks were noticeably worse with additional symptoms. I got intensely sensitive to light and sound and became so nauseated that it was touch and go as to whether I would get sick. The pain of the last two migraines had reached a whole new level. It began around my right eye and traveled to the back of my head and down my neck. The throbbing I experienced brought me to tears. I took one Imitrex, another one an hour later, and experienced no relief at all. I ended up waiting as long as I could and planned to take another one a few hours later. Although the prescription called for no more than two Imitrex in 24 hours, I just couldn't stand the pain. These migraines lasted for at least two days instead of a few hours.

I felt worried because I knew I should be packing and cleaning instead of lying there in my bed doing nothing. Also, my daughter's graduation was the next day, and I was concerned that I would still be experiencing the same amount of pain.

After lots of praying and lots of medicine, I woke feeling better that Saturday morning. I still had some pain, but it was nothing compared to the day before. I took an Imitrex with my morning coffee.

Carleigh and I were getting ready together in my bathroom. We put on makeup and did our hair as we talked. As I was telling my daughter about all I had to do, I could feel the stress and the tears I had been holding in begin to inundate me. The more I talked, the more I wanted to cry. I could feel my heart beating faster. The pounding in my head returned. My emotions were bubbling to the surface. Then I stopped myself. For the love of God, this was a big day for my daughter, her high school graduation. This day would only come once. I stopped myself and I apologized to her. I hugged her and told her I loved her and that I was so proud of her.

The streets of downtown Raleigh were gridlocked. After we arrived, we found the Raleigh Convention Center bustling with thousands of people. Family members who hadn't seen each other in a while greeted and hugged each other along with friends there to show their support. Young people wearing purple caps and gowns rushed through the crowd to get to their spots in the procession line. The group that graduated before Carleigh's class filed out of the convention center as we were all making our way into the building. There was a long line of ticket holders.

I was so thankful that my good friend Pam was there with me. Bryce and Carleigh's boyfriend, Kevin, volunteered to park the car so we could get everyone's tickets to them. Dozens of people strolled the sidewalks, making their way through the large glass doors that led into the convention center. About 50 feet in front of us, I saw two adorable, dark-haired little girls twirling and talking. These two cuties were my nieces, Catherine and Brooklynn. On a bench off to the left, their mom, my sister-in-law Lisa, sat with her husband, Marc. I said my first hellos to my cute nieces; Lisa gave me a tight hug as did Marc. I introduced Pam to them. A few moments later, my kids' grandparents showed up. They both gave me tight hugs, expressing their condolences about my dad's passing.

As we gave our tickets to the attendants, we moved down the stairs to the enormous warehouse-looking room where the ceremony would take place. The room was concrete and cement; large fluorescent lights and fans hung from the high ceiling. Row upon row of folding chairs lined the floor. There was a large stage with several chairs and a podium. Big screens were strategically positioned so family members and friends could get an up-close view of their graduate walking across the stage to receive their diploma.

My heart overflowed with joy as I watched my daughter cross the stage—a big, beautiful smile on her face. I experienced so many emotions. I felt pride for my daughter and all of her hard work and accomplishments. I felt happiness, joy, excitement, and, yes, sadness too. Just two short years earlier, my dad had been there with us to celebrate my son's graduation. Now, there was an empty chair and an empty place in my heart. I knew he was watching us from above, but I would have given anything to have him there with me. *I miss you, Dad, so much.*

At the end of our celebration that day, my heart and my stomach were full! The day was beautiful. My daughter graduated and soon would begin a new, exciting chapter in her life. I got to spend some time with family and a dear friend. The lunch I had was fabulous, and the vegan cake my daughter recommended blew everyone away—scrumptious!

By late afternoon, I was home again. It was a typical North Carolina June day, warm with the humidity at a tolerable 70 percent. God had given us another Carolina blue sky. A slight breeze in the air kept the heat from feeling claustrophobic. A few hours later, and I was relaxing in bed, enjoying a cup of coffee and a movie. I had just spoken to Will, and my heart was full from the day of fun, family, and love.

"Goodnight, Dad," I whispered. I reached to turn off my light and then snuggled under my soft down comforter. I folded my hands in prayer. I prayed and said goodnight to my dad as I did every night. I prayed that he heard me and was smiling down on us.

A few days passed, and I slowly began making progress on packing things up in my house. Carleigh and I made a trip to the Guardian Angel, a local secondhand store that took donations. All of their proceeds went to Alzheimer's research. It seemed that, as I cleaned one room, another filled up with boxes and bags of stuff that would either be donated or eventually brought to my dad's house. Our large bonus room, 12 by 12 feet, was still jampacked with boxes and bags. I could barely get in the room. I had yet to gather the courage to tackle that room. Looking around, that space full of things to be donated and the rest of the house were messy and disorganized. Nothing seemed in place.

My dad's house was even more disorganized and cluttered than mine. Bryce and I first started putting things that we weren't sure whether to keep or donate in my dad's bedroom. We cleaned out the other two bedrooms for him and Carleigh. But by this point my dad's room was full of furniture, lamps, boxes and boxes of pictures and photo albums, and other miscellaneous items. Walking down the hallway in my dad's house, I saw the red USMC hat that hung on the doorknob to his bedroom. I smiled and opened the door. "Good morning, Dad," I said each morning when I walked into his bedroom. I stopped and stared at the mess before me. My mind said, "Ugh." I already felt defeated and overwhelmed with thoughts of cleaning out this room. How would I ever clear out this entire house in time for us to move our stuff in?

My dad's computer room, which would be Carleigh's bedroom, was once clean and organized. Now, it was full to the brim with bags and boxes to be donated. So I had two rooms that were a disaster. Where would I begin? Thankfully, my best friend from New Jersey, Arrie, would be there in one day, and she would be a huge help.

Chapter 8: New Beginnings

I had just finished my dinner, which consisted of jasmine rice, black beans, and roasted chicken. With each bite, our two black labs, Braxton and Ryder, patiently sat and watched intently every morsel that made it into my mouth and, unfortunately, not on the floor. Braxton, our boy, is a small version of a Great Dane. His jowls were wet from drooling with every bite I took. Ryder, our girl, is smaller, looks more like a Lab except that her fur is more of a brindle color. She sat so perfectly like a lady, her posture perfect, giving full attention to my every move. She sat at a greater distance than Braxton to avoid upsetting me. Braxton, on the other hand, has no concept of boundaries. He was right next to me, his nose wiggling. I heard his slight, short inhales as he tried to be good. His anxious nose nudged the edge of my plate. Knowing I would be disciplining him at any moment, he couldn't help but to sneak a lick, all the while looking right at me.

I heard a loud rumbling outside, the sound of a noisy exhaust as a car pulled into our street. The noise drew the dogs' attention. Without hesitation, they abandoned me and ran to the front door for a closer look. Their barking became louder and more frequent as I heard this roaring engine pull into my driveway.

The myth, the mystery, the legend, my friend Arrie had arrived. I opened the front door so the dogs could release their excitement and greet her. In my driveway sat a beautiful, classic, bright red T-top Corvette, detailed to the nines. Any description would fail to do it justice. The license plate read, "XCELR8."

I walked out of the house to greet Arrie and we hugged tightly and long. It had been at least seven or eight years since we had seen each other. She is *the friend*—the kind we all have—with whom we can pick right up where we left off even after months without talking. We have been through so much together and have loved and supported each other through it all.

I've said it a thousand times before, but she is truly one of the smartest and strongest people I know. God truly blessed me the day she walked into my life. Arrie is this fun, spirited, funny as hell, endearing, loving, and brutally honest friend. She has been there for me for the past 28 years. I am a better person for having her in my life.

"Oh, my God, have I missed you." I said to her as we hugged. All smiles, looking at each other, we took in how much we had changed since the last time we saw each other. We both had more wrinkles, more experience, and more life behind us.

"Damn, we have *a lot* of catching up to do!" I said.

She was visiting from New Jersey. She had driven down to be with me during this difficult time and also to help me pack, clean, and do some painting in my dad's house. After our hellos and a tour through my house to show her what needed to be done before it went on the market, my kids trickled in to welcome her.

They freakin' love Arrie! She is a funny, storytelling, cussing, no holds barred on what she says, can always laugh at herself type of person. My kids were captivated by her smile, her laugh, her car, and her stories. She lit up the room. They both had met her several times in the past when I would visit family and friends in New Jersey. But they were older now and enjoyed her enthusiasm on a different, more mature level.

We sat and talked all night. I knew she was exhausted from the 10-hour drive, and I, well, I was always tired! After a few hours of catching up, we decided to call it a night. Arrie would only be there for a few days, and we had a lot to do in that time.

The next morning, Thursday, June 14, as quietly as possible, I crept past Arrie, who was sleeping on our couch in the living room, and walked into the kitchen to make a pot of coffee. Knowing that both of us loved our morning cup of Joe, making coffee was a top priority on our to-do list for the day.

"Good morning," Arrie said as she sleepily made her way into the kitchen.

"Sleep okay?" I asked.

"Yeah, okay." I could tell she was as tired as I was, but we had too much to do that day to blow off our plans.

After a few hours of talking, we finally headed to the local Home Depot and purchased supplies for our home improvement projects. Finally arriving at my dad's house, I opened the door and Goober came running down the front stairs to greet our guest. Being the animal lover that she is and Goober being the sweetest boy ever, Arrie instantly fell in love with him.

The feeling of being overwhelmed hit me the moment I walked through the front door. The house was in disarray. I looked around and saw disorganization. The place was filled with boxes and bags of things to get thrown out or donated. Nothing appeared clean. I had a sinking feeling in my stomach.

"Okay, where do we start?" Arrie asked.

I showed her the kitchen cabinets. Throughout my dad's house, the cabinets were a yellowish oak color, and we planned to paint them to update their appearance. I gave her a brief tour of the house, which took no more than a few minutes. My dad's house was a small but adorable place.

"I'll start with these," Arrie announced as she staked a claim to the hall bathroom. Without a moment's hesitation, she started breaking open the paintbrushes, pan, and paint. She set herself up and got to work immediately. We decided to paint all the cabinets with chalk paint in black. We would sand them a bit to give them a weathered look, lacquer them to give them a shine, and replace the fixtures with brushed silver knobs.

Begrudgingly, I made my way down the hall to my dad's room. I could no longer put off cleaning out these rooms. But I didn't know where to begin. It seemed like all I was doing was relocating things from one room to another. With a heavy sigh and a roll of my eyes (I am a Jersey Girl, after all), I decided to go through the drawers in my dad's bedroom furniture. Once I got started, it was easy. I donated most of my dad's clothes. I put the bags and boxes to be donated in the room that would become Carleigh's bedroom. The garage became the storage space for stuff to go to the dump.

By dinner time, Arrie and I were busting our humps to get things done, and I felt amazingly accomplished. Standing in the hallway, looking at both rooms, I could see the progress I'd made. Carleigh's room was full of things to be donated, but finally my dad's room was slowly being cleaned out and there was some walking room. I decide to list some of my dad's bedroom furniture as well as some chairs and tables in the living room on Facebook Marketplace to free up some space and make room for my furniture.

Within the first few hours, I had several offers on my dad's furniture. Just three days later, by the time Arrie left, I had sold about 10 pieces, freed up a bunch of space in my dad's place, and made a little money to boot.

The days that Arrie was there were wonderful. I got to spend some much-needed time with a cherished friend. We talked a lot as we always did. Arrie is one of those friends that you can share anything with, knowing it will go no further, and there was never any judgment. We did lots of laughing, some crying, but it was all needed; it was all good. When she left on Saturday, my dad's bedroom and the living room were almost empty. Every single cabinet in my dad's house had been refinished, and the hall bathroom had a fresh coat of paint. We worked all day every day from about 7:00 or so in the morning until 10:00 or 11:00 at night.

At 10:00 on Saturday night, Arrie left and made the drive back to New Jersey. We hugged tightly before she got into the car. I was already missing her. Goober and I watched as she drove off.

Back inside, I locked the door behind us. It was way too quiet for me. With Arrie there, the place was filled with so much life, the sounds of us talking, hammering, painting, moving furniture, and packing. Now, there was nothing but the low hum of the refrigerator. Smiling, I walked through each room, inspecting the work Arrie had done. It looked new, fresh, and different. My dad said on more than one occasion that he wanted me to make his place my own. I finally could see the small changes that were making this place feel a little more like mine. I walked down the hall to my dad's room and turned on the light. It felt good to see the room open, the clutter gone. I envisioned my furniture in this room and smiled. At that moment, I felt happy with the progress.

"Good night, Dad," I said turning off the light and closing his door. Exhausted, I knew I was going to sleep well that night.

By the last Wednesday in June, Dad's house was finally taking shape and looking less cluttered. I slowly began bringing things from my house. Keeping to what had become a daily routine,

I decided to take a break and have a cup of coffee around 3:00 in the afternoon. The day was a typical hot, steamy, Southern summer day, a balmy 96 degrees. I took a sip of my coffee and sat next to Goober. He was in his usual spot on the couch, and the moment I sat down, he moved closer and snuggled with me. I turned on the TV. I didn't really care what I was watching. I just wanted something mindless to take a break from all the cleaning and packing.

On the mantle above the fireplace sat a small 3" x 5" black frame, outlining a black and white photo of a young, handsome man. He wasn't smiling; he had a look of purpose and appeared stern yet approachable. It was only a headshot, but his posture was clearly erect, his head tilted so slightly towards the left. In this picture, my dad was dressed in full Marine uniform. It was his graduation photo. Out of the thousands of photographs we had, this was my absolute *favorite* of my dad. I took a moment to admire it from where Goober and I were chilling.

In that moment, from the corner of my eye, something caught my attention. Below the mantle, on the ceramic fireplace surround, a small brown roach scurried across the tile. Ew! What a disgusting little creature with its six legs, long antennae, and shiny brown outer coating. I imagined all the dirt and multitude of germs it carried all over its disgusting body. My skin crawled. That was all it took for me to call the local exterminator we had been using for my own house for years.

As a result of the roach experience, I learned that my dad's house had termites! It took all day and quite a bit of money for the exterminator to treat the house for roaches, ants, and spiders. In the process of ridding the house of creepy crawlers, they also found mold in the crawl space. The news just kept getting worse. At the end of what was likely a long day for the exterminator and his partner, Dad's house was free of bugs and mold.

On Sunday, July 8, I woke up exhausted. Sleep eluded me that night. Ever so slowly, we were making progress on cleaning and packing. On top of everything I had to do with packing, donating, moving, and selling my house, there was one more thing I needed to do.

There is nothing like learning something you have absolutely not a single inkling about and are clueless about where to start. My dad's will presented a challenge since I had never dealt with anything like that. I felt overwhelmed and frustrated because I already had so much on my plate, but I had to face this job. My parents were not rich by any stretch of the imagination. With that said, they were both hard workers, saving when they could. My dad was one of the hardest working people I ever knew. He worked any job that paid the bills and put food on the table. He was proud of what he did regardless of the type of job. Years past, he spent some time with my Uncle Al and learned a few things about investing. My uncle was a smart man, and, from what my dad told me, he was a very frugal man who saved every penny and invested well. The end result was that my dad was able to leave me a little something—not much—but a small amount to help me with expenses, retirement, and college for his grandkids. True to himself, my dad was conservative when it came to money and worried about taking care of me right up to his last breath.

Those who have dealt with the process of having a will probated will relate to my experience. I learned that patience was key. I contacted the lawyer that drew up my parents' will. This wonderful, sweet lady, Ms. Rhodes, was instrumental in helping me figure out the legalities of it all. Generally, to the best of my understanding, when a will is probated, the county clerk reviews it and makes sure there are no other beneficiaries, that the documentation is legal and binding, and basically that there are no kinks. Once the will is probated, Letters of Testamentary are written. To the best of my understanding, these are letters that basically state who the beneficiary is and that this person or persons have a legal right to the deceased loved one's property or belongings.

I had to send these Letters of Testamentary to the various small investments my dad had, life insurance, home and car insurance, etc. Literally *nothing* could get done until these individuals had this document in hand, so I patiently waited. The will had been in probate since the beginning of June, and, even though there was so much to do, I couldn't get anything done until those damn letters were in my hands. Anyone who has lost a loved one and who is a beneficiary in that loved one's will has to complete what is called a "Transfer of Death" packet if that loved one had investments. I really *hate* that wording. Basically, this is a packet of a dozen or so pages that requires a flurry of financial and personal information, a death certificate, Letters of Testamentary, and information about how you want to receive the funds. The beneficiary needs to mail each packet individually to each investment and wait. And wait and wait and wait. This can be frustrating if you are not a fan of patience or have a life to live.

I found that prayer was life-saving as it is with anything in life. Admittedly, I had been worrying so much about the unknown since my dad's death. I am a person of strong faith, and yet I worried, which made me feel like a hypocrite. I knew God was in control or at least I should have known, yet I was losing sleep and feeling anxiety and worry. I enlisted my closest prayer warriors to pray for me. When my thoughts started to run away with the "what if" scenarios, I stopped, took a breath, and prayed.

I worried about how I was going to pay for everything and about when my house would sell. Many questions ran through my mind: What if there were expensive items on the punch list after the house was inspected? How was I going to pay for Carleigh's college and things for her dorm? I needed to take time off to take her to school, but I had no vacation days left after using them all when my dad was sick. How were the animals going to adjust to the move? I hoped the budget I was responsible for at work balanced. I left suddenly during my department's year-end to take care of my dad, and I worried about what I would return to. I worried about my kids, their schooling, health, etc. I struggled with the idea of missing Carleigh when she was finally out of the nest and off to school. The list went on, and there were times when I couldn't turn off my mind.

Although it seemed like I was busy and stressed 24/7, that was not totally true. I did get some down time and spent those moments going to church or movies with my daughter, making my son's favorite home-cooked meal, and enjoying good conversations with my kids, who were now adults themselves. The occasional glass of chardonnay accompanied me while Carleigh and I watched *The Bachelorette*. I tried to find some *me time* when I could. Through all of this, I had moments of mourning too. I caught myself thinking, "I have to call Dad and tell him this, and he'll crack up." I looked at pictures and listened to his voicemails that I had saved.

Driving in my car the other day, the song "Love Will Keep Us Together" from the duo Captain and Tennille came on the radio, and I cried. Tears fell for a long time, yet I was smiling. This song was popular and had a lot of airtime when I was nine. It is tied to some joyful memories of my family making the long drive on Route 95 South to Florida for our yearly vacation. Hearing it brought me back to sitting in the back of our emerald green, two-door Ford Pinto. Without air conditioning in the car, all the windows were rolled down to cool us on those hot summer days. The air blew through the car tossing my white-blond hair around my face. The humidity and heat felt almost suffocating, and the air smelled of hot tar and exhaust. Both of my parents were smoking a cigarette. My dad was driving; my mother never drove. Well, she did once when my dad was tired from being on the road for so long; he pulled over at a rest stop, they switched seats, and my mom readjusted the driver's seat and mirrors and started backing out of the rest stop.

My dad firmly reminded her, "All you have to do is stay on Route 95 *South*," accentuating the word "south." "Don't turn off anywhere; just keep going *south*."

She nodded, confirming her understanding of his instructions. My dad watched and waited until we were once again on Route 95 South. Finally able to relax, he reclined his seat all the way back, got comfortable, and quickly fell asleep. I remember nodding off shortly after he did.

I don't know how much time had gone by when I heard my dad yelling, "Damn it, Elaine! Why are we heading north?!"

At the age of nine, you're not really paying attention to all the details of the road, all you know is you're heading towards your vacation destination, and you will be promptly informed when you have arrived. Route 95 could be a tedious road to travel and a lot of the topography looked the same. However, I was old enough to read, and I was pretty sure we had passed the Delaware sign earlier that day, and, yep, we passed it again. I don't know how she did it. She needed to do one thing: stay on the highway she was already on. The rest of that ride, needless to say, was quiet and tense.

The other day Carleigh and I were talking about college in the same way she and her boyfriend discussed their future. She was so happy, things in her life were going well, this was an exciting time as she prepared to start a new chapter, and she had so much to look forward to. I caught myself thinking of my dad during our conversation. As happy and excited as I was for my daughter, I was struck by a wave of sadness at the thought that my dad wouldn't be there to see her graduate from college or watch Carleigh get married. The realization hit me that I wouldn't be able to call my dad and talk to him on that long drive home from Maryland after I dropped Carleigh off at school. Moments like those where I get caught up in thoughts of what would never be with my dad made me realize just how much I missed him.

I couldn't think too long about certain things or I would break down, which I'd done a lot of lately. I would never again get to hug my dad and feel the softness of his flannel shirt and the scruffiness of his five o'clock shadow or smell the distinct aroma of cigarettes and coffee on his breath. These things were my dad, and I missed them to the point where they easily brought tears to my eyes and a tightness in my throat.

I missed hearing, "Hey, Cyn," and even little, seemingly insignificant things like his cough or the shuffle of his feet as he walked, the sound and smell of him lighting a cigarette, the beep of his handheld poker game, the way he would hum while he made breakfast, or tap his fingers on the tabletop to the rhythm of *The Lone Ranger* theme song. I missed him saying to Carleigh, "How's my little girl?" and all of his one-liners. The list of all of those uniquely Dad moments that now lived only in my memory was long.

As I went through what I had written so far, as I read, edited, removed and changed some of the wording, one thing stood out like a beacon in a storm: I started my journal referring to my dad in the present tense. It was numbing to realize he was no longer with us. As I read what I wrote on those first few pages, I could never fathom all that I would experience or imagine how it all would unfold. I couldn't comprehend the depth of my emotions as I watched my dad's health decline. I had assumed he would be there for my daughter's graduation. Looking back at my words, I expected I would be able to cook him these big, flavorful meals. Instead, I watched his appetite diminish until he was barely eating anything at the end. The kids and I had even considered surprising him with a four-day cruise to the Bahamas at the end of May, ironically right around the time he died.

On Monday, July 16, 2018, I resumed my *normal* life and schedule and returned to work as Assistant to the Dean at a local community college. I loved my job and my coworkers. It would be good to get back to my regular routine and not have my mind overloaded and occupied with all of the things I had been dealing with during those past few weeks and months. Normalcy was a wonderful thing.

Things in my life were slowly coming together. I had made some progress with getting our house ready to put on the market and sell. We had received a contingency offer awaiting the appraisal and inspection. I was also slowly moving things over to my dad's house, which would become my house in the next few weeks.

My kids were doing great. Bryce decided to pursue a degree in nursing. He planned to finish his two-year associate degree at the college where I worked and pursue his Bachelor of Science in nursing at UNC Charlotte. I would be taking Carleigh to MICA on August 21 for orientation.

Will and I were doing great as well. He had been such a blessing and my rock through this journey.

My friends were all there for me in one way or another. The incredible women God had brought into my life were all special. Life was good.

The sale of my house I once shared with my ex-husband, the house where my kids grew up, would be finalized at the end of August. If all went well, we would close on August 29. I slowly continued to bring my things over to my dad's house, making the home ours.

I was also gradually making progress on all of the paperwork and financial things for my dad's personal affairs. As each day passed, I began to see more light at the end of the tunnel. I was feeling less stressed and more accomplished as the days passed. I stopped and realized that it had been two months since my dad passed. Those eight weeks had gone by in a blink of an eye yet his passing remained frozen in time in my memory.

On August 26, 2018, I reopened my journal a few weeks after returning to work and resuming my normal life and routine. It had been four weeks since I last journaled.

As expected, I had been busy with lots of things going on and moving along. The first offer on my house fell through, so we were still having many showings. I anticipated an offer soon. With the house on the market, the rooms were decluttered. I'd donated countless bags of items we were ready to let go, and I continued to make sure the house was clean and show-ready. Bryce was living in my dad's house. He helped with the painting, yardwork, and basic maintenance. Our dogs were also staying with him, which made keeping my house clean for potential buyers easy and stress-free.

Last week we drove Carleigh to college in Maryland. It was a bittersweet trip. I watched my kids interact and actually get along—go figure! Bryce was a huge help with moving her in and just being there for me for the long drive home. I was worried about that drive and so thankful I had my son with me. I was trying to get familiar with having an empty house to come home to. I still had to pinch myself and realize just how fast the time had gone. Twenty years of parenting flew by as did those months from the moment my dad was diagnosed till his death. In just a few days, it would be three months since he left us.

The level of loss and change in my life at times left me feeling a deep longing for the way things used to be, for the days when my daughter was just in the next room and my father was just a five-minute drive away. If my dad were still here, he would have listened to me rant about my daughter being gone and would have given me words of wisdom or a strong shoulder to cry on. He would have said something to make me laugh and reminded me that I was made of sturdy stock. He was my person. As much as I loved my fiancé, my kids, and my friends, I knew I would always miss the man who made me who I am.

For now, I waited patiently for my house to sell. I was ready to move to New Bern to be with Will and begin this next chapter of my life with the man I love. Although I absolutely loved the people I worked with and the job I had, I was ready to look for another position. Saying goodbye to my work friends would be the toughest part about leaving, but I was excited to get a little place of my own and make it feel like home in a quaint, historical coastal town. And I was eager to start sharing my daily life with Will. The only thing missing would be my dad, but he would want me to live my life fully and joyfully.

On Friday, September 14, 2018, the sky was gray and trees were swaying, tossed about by strong winds. The ground was already saturated from recent rains. The wind subsided as I enjoyed my morning cup of coffee and watched some TV, waiting for Hurricane Florence to make her full arrival. As of 8:41 a.m., we were experiencing the outer bands of this enormous storm. I was as ready as I was ever going to be. I had lots of food, ice, water, flashlights, and electronics fully charged. The tub was filled with water in the event we lost power. We were expecting power outages, trees down, and flooding. I'd lived in North Carolina for over 20 years, and in that time I had experienced Hurricanes Fran, Floyd, and Matthew to name a few. Each one left its marks from extensive flooding, downed trees, power outages, tornados, and loss of life. I'll never forget any of these storms. My body tensed as the wind picked up and blew harder.

We had this beautiful, three-trunk river birch that stood about 50-60 feet tall and grew close to the corner of my house. Its canopy covered the corner of my bedroom. The thought of losing that beautiful tree saddened me. I would hate even worse for it to fall and land on my house and my bedroom.

The impending hurricane was what I would consider the first big event where my dad wasn't here. If he were there, I felt positive he would be braving the storm from his porch, cup of coffee and cigarette in tow. I would have gotten the occasional phone call from him checking in to see how I was holding up during the storm. Now he was my protector in a different way, watching over me in spirit.

We made it through Hurricane Florence and were lucky to have no damage and minimal power outages. Other parts of the state and the Eastern seaboard didn't fare so well. New Bern, North Carolina, a quaint historic town, got hit hardest by the hurricane. Our 36-foot Catalina sailboat was docked there, and the marina was almost destroyed. The water level exceeded 20 feet, throwing a lot of the boats at the marina on top of the docks and on each other. The main building that housed the recreation room, bathrooms, showers, laundry room and offices was completely flooded almost to the second floor. Power was out all along the coast, and we couldn't get there for days because of the flooding and trees and downed powerlines. Once we were able to make our way to the coast and check on our boat, we found that, by the grace of God, she was spared. She didn't have a scratch on her. She sat perfectly straight in her slip. It was difficult to drive through the town and backroads and see the destruction of so many homes, boats, roads, and local businesses.

Chapter 9: Mirror Image

As time passes, I notice how much I really am like my father, not in terms of physical appearance but in all of the little things, our habits, beliefs, likes and dislikes. Some of these behaviors, I've passed on to my kids.

Driving in the mountains of Northwestern New Jersey, we had to be aware of our surroundings and keep an eye out for deer. Herds of them roamed the area as soon as dusk appeared. As a child, I remember sitting in the passenger seat, barely big enough to see above the dashboard when my dad said, "Don't forget to look around. What are we looking for?" My dad would glance at me sitting at attention, eyes wide, darting from one side of the road to the other, my skinny little legs crossed beneath me. Sitting this way gave me a little boost so I could see a bit more over the dashboard.

I knew exactly what he was referring to. If you kept your eyes open and happened to be driving on any road in Sussex County at that time of day, you were guaranteed to see deer grazing along the side of the road. The trick was watching for that moment when the deer lifted their heads momentarily from their feeding and their eyes reflected a bright yellow in the car headlights. That's what my dad quizzed me about. Anyone with good eyesight could spot those two small, circular, bright-yellow reflections from a distance. If we were lucky (well, I considered it lucky), we would see dozens of those little yellow light flashes staring back at us as we went by.

To this day, when I'm driving with my daughter around dusk, I don't need to say a word. "I know; look for deer," she says, and a slight grin appears on my face. My dad taught us well.

My daughter has always mentioned that I take really good care of her when she's sick. She always says she wants her mom. I realize that most of us want our moms when we aren't feeling well. For me, it was my dad. He had that uncanny way of making me feel comforted and calm. He had a lot of self-taught medical knowledge. Most of it came from growing up in a household with two nurses, and he passed that on to me. Thinking back, maybe I am giving him a little too much credit. My grandmother and aunt were excellent nurses, and they instilled a ton of what they knew in him, which he apparently passed on to me. So, whenever my kids were sick, I always loved taking care of them just like my dad did for me.

Oh, how I hate the cold! The *only* way I can stand the winter is being inside the house, snuggled up in my favorite chair under lots of blankets by a fire, watching the beautiful snow as it falls. As a child, I loved the snow. What kid doesn't love playing in the snow until they are chilled to the bone? I took so much joy at coming inside to sit by the fireplace and sip a cup of hot chocolate as I thawed out. I recall several times when my dad said, "Snow is fun when you're young. It's not so much fun when you have to shovel it and drive in it." No truer words were ever spoken.

I not only despise frigid weather, I can't tolerate any kind of cold. If I get even a slight chill, I go from feeling comfortable to my fingertips and toes freezing and even a touch of numbness.

My feet are *always* cold—even in summer. My dad always complained about the same thing. Thanks, Dad. I could've done without this one physical trait.

Just like my dad, I have always been partial to warmer temperatures and weather. I adore sunny days and the sounds and smells of spring and summer—the ocean breeze, the rustling of palm trees moved by the wind, and the sight of Spanish moss swaying. I believe the reason for this is twofold. Taking so many trips to Florida when I was young gave me so many wonderful, happy memories. But I also think I just love the sunshine. I am one of those people whose mood is directly related to the weather. Rainy day, gloomy Cyndi. Sunny day, happy, happy Cyndi.

Another gift from my dad that lives on in me is an enthusiasm for cars. It's commonplace for many men to have some working knowledge about cars, their engines, and their general maintenance. Thankfully, I have passed on to my kids some of this knowledge my dad instilled in me. Both of my kids were lucky (or unlucky) enough to inherit my old Chrysler Pacifica. By the time they drove it, it had at least 125,000 miles on it and was burning through oil. On more than one occasion, when the oil level got too low, the Pacifica fail-safe feature automatically shut off the engine and the steering wheel locked. This kept the car from being run without oil, which seizes the engine. It still allowed the driver to slowly get off the road. (Anyone who knows anything about cars is aware that, if you run an engine without oil and it seizes, you're looking at rebuilding the transmission, which is costly.) Both of my kids knew to always have an extra quart or two of oil with them and have on more than one occasion had to pop the hood and add a quart.

Need versus want: How many of us truly know the difference and live by it? My dad instilled this value in me, always drilled it into me, exhaustively.

As I've typed this book, pausing and re-reading, I've gotten the strongest scent of my dad. It's even on my hands like I've been at his house for days. It's the smell of hard work, of engine grease, of cigarettes and coffee, of the old flannel shirt he used to wear, of all the things that remind me of my dad. It brings back all the feelings of home that came with the presence of my dad. I love you, Dad. I know you're nearby and watching over me.

Chapter 10: Old Wounds

The process of writing this memoir has been healing for me. Throughout my life, I have always been daddy's little girl. He was first and foremost my father, but, once I was an adult with my own life, he became my friend, my *best* friend. We had the greatest relationship, and I miss him terribly.

My relationship with my mom, however, is a completely different story. Growing up, especially in my teen years, several of my friends would say, "My mom and I have the best relationship. We are so close. I tell my mom everything." I would think, "Really?" That wasn't the case with me and my mom. We never got along, not until I was into my thirties. We didn't see eye to eye on anything, and I didn't want to be anything like her. We also had several big disagreements in my adult years. Horrible, I know, but I'm being honest.

I blamed my mom for a lot of things. At times, she would say or do things that a mom just shouldn't say or do to their child. I always felt a strong disconnect between the two of us. I struggled to get close to her.

Twelve years after her passing, I have finally moved on and have forgiven my mom. She wasn't perfect. None of us are. We walk through this life with personality flaws, emotional damage and baggage, insecurities. My mom was no different. It took me decades to finally be at peace with the person my mom was as a mother, a wife, a daughter, and a friend.

My mother died on December 8, 2006, twelve years before my dad. I clearly remember the day she died and the weeks that followed. One memory vividly sticks in my mind: Christmas Day, 2006, the first Christmas without my mom. For years, we always celebrated Christmas Eve at my mom and dad's house. Christmas Day was always a quiet day at home, so the kids could enjoy the goodies Santa left for them. This year was different. I couldn't bear the thought the thought of my dad being alone on Christmas Day the first year without my mom and her passing so close to the holiday. That Christmas Day was unlike any other. Of course, we celebrated, we ate, we opened gifts, and like every year we watched *A Christmas Story*. My dad was never one to become overly emotional about anything. Even though we had a nice day, there was an obvious void, a loss that was somber, dark, sad, and screamingly evident.

My dad went home around 8:30 that night. He said his goodbyes to all of us. He held a few gift bags in one hand and a handled paper bag in the other hand that contained a slice or two of my apple pie and a few containers with enough leftovers for a week. I walked him to the front door and gave him a kiss and a hug goodnight. I watched him carefully make his way down our front stoop and walk, alone, without my mom, for the first time ever on Christmas. He walked down our driveway in the dark, cold December air. He got into his car and left. I stood there at my front door, and through the window I watched his every move. He backed out of our driveway and drove away. He went home to an empty house, to go to bed alone and wake up alone. My heart was aching with tremendous sadness for him. He looked so alone in those moments. The tears easily came; there was no fighting them. Twelve years later and this memory and the emotions I felt back then remain so vivid and strong.

When I look back on my childhood, my dad is a part of most of my happy memories. My mom was a worrier. She viewed everything from a glass half empty perspective. She tended to be a martyr, always focusing on the worst case scenario and sure that the worst possible outcome would happen. No matter how big or small the situation was, it was worst case for her, and the universe was out to get her. It was hard for her to relax and *just be*. As much as I hate to admit it, I inherited some of those traits. I am well aware of them and fight to change them.

My mom's struggle with the glass half-empty outlook was engrained in her growing up. But I personally believe she wrestled with depression. She wasn't a huge advocate of doctor visits, so she was never clinically diagnosed, but looking back now, having observed her behavior firsthand, I truly feel she had some form of depression.

When all was said and done, I believe that my mom did the best she could. She loved the best she could. She dealt with life's ups and downs to the best of her ability. She forgave as well as she could.

At this point in my life, I'm a middle-aged, divorced mom working full-time towards my retirement. I've experienced happy times and times of loss and sadness while raising two teenagers and dealing with the everyday stresses of life. I believe happiness is a choice. Seeing the glass as half full is a choice. I do my best, yet I know I fall short, and I am a work in progress. I pray, I seek, I try, and I struggle at times. I don't always choose happiness. I can be a martyr. I worry. I stress. I get angry. So did my mom. She didn't rely on her faith like I do; she wore her scars and hurts on her sleeve and heart. It breaks my heart to know that she lived her 68 years this way when happiness was always within her reach if she chose it. I forgive her. I love her and miss her. The biggest comfort? Knowing that my mom and dad are finally together again, and they will be guardian angels for my children and me for the rest of our days.

The year 2018 was a time I will truly never forget. I experienced love, happiness, laughter, fear, heartache, loss, and struggles that a year or a few months prior I could never have anticipated let alone think I would survive. I've experienced it all. It has taught me so much.

Yes, I have so much to be thankful for. So much has happened, lots of good, happy things. My life is moving forward in a positive, exciting way. I know my dad is watching over me, over all of us, and smiling, even laughing.

Epilogue

I wrote this memoir first and foremost for myself. I wanted to have something tangible I could actually look back at over the years that could refresh my memory of my childhood, my mom, and my dad. I wanted to be able to laugh, cry, and say to myself, "Holy crap, I totally forgot about that!"

As I began this journey of journaling about my dad, I truly didn't realize all he had done for me as a parent, as a papa to my kids, and as a friend. Some of what I've shared in these pages might seem trivial, maybe not even worth mentioning. But this was a personal journey for me. As I've read and re-read this a thousand times, I realize there is something else I hope will be taken from this book. I hope you will take a close, honest look at your own childhood, your life, and at those people who made an impact, good or bad. Remember all those moments shared with best friends, first loves, your favorite teacher, coach, mentor, sibling, grandparent, pastor, doctor, parent. Think back to that first kiss and heartbreak. Let's not forget to give an honorable mention to the people you wanted to smack silly or even beat the crap out of: the bully, the mean kid, the teacher that disregarded you, or that person who made you feel stupid, unimportant, not needed. I hope you will examine all those small, minute moments in time and those monumental, stand-out, larger-than-life memories that changed your life and made you who you are. For me, one person was constant in those memories, and that person was my dad.

After you read the last sentence and close this book, I hope you have a heart and mind full of memories and love, reminiscences that brought you back and made you a kid again at least for a paragraph or a page, made you smile, laugh, maybe cry, or even forgive someone. If this book gives you the opportunity to move past old hurts, then I consider it a huge success.

This memoir is also for those who have had to watch someone they love die. It's for those of you who took care of your loved one, who stood strong during the difficult times, who cried when you could but carried on because you had to. God bless you. You have lived through probably one of the most difficult times in your life. My prayer is that even through the sadness, grieving, and loss, you find the love, peace, and happiness that you deserve and that your loved one wants for you.

One day, we will all leave this Earth. We can't fake our way out of it, pray it away, or hope it never happens. However, if you can give someone the gift of love, peace, forgiveness, whatever you may call it or whatever you and your loved ones need, I think that's a true blessing. If we can all leave this earth knowing we mattered, we made a difference, then every hurt, laugh, tear, pain, and memory happened for a reason. Somewhere along the way, you made an impact. My dad made a *huge* impact, not just with me but also on my kids, on some of the kids who grew up on our street, and on his friends.

Thank you, Dad. Thank you for raising me; thank you for being the best dad a daughter could *ever* ask for. Thank you for teaching me how to be a strong, independent woman. Thank you for sharing your love of nature and animals. Thank you for teaching me the difference between needs and wants. Thank you for being the best Papa to my kids. Thank you for teaching me how to fish and how to shoot a gun. Thank you for instilling in me the love of history and enjoying the simple things in life. Thank you for the hundreds of happy memories I have from my childhood and beyond. Most of all, thank you for letting me share the last two months of your life with you. Every word, every breath, every ache, every pain, every smile, every tear, every memory. And thank you for showing me what it means to die with dignity, humility, and grace.

Dad, I miss you terribly. Not a day, an hour, a moment goes by that I don't think of you in some way. There is a huge void in my life without you here. I've listened to your voice messages that I have saved on my phone. I miss the sound of your voice. You had reached out to me every few days just to see how things were going. You were always active in mine and my kids' lives. You always gave me and my kids sound advice. Along with the sadness I feel now, there is an overflowing heart full of gratitude, love, and joy because I had 50 wonderful years with my dad.

Until I see you again, I know you'll be watching over me and your grandkids, guiding us, loving us. As you told me a million times while you were here, "Don't worry about things you can't change." So, I wait (patiently) for my house to sell while trying to figure out where the second part of my life will take me, where Carleigh will end up in her pursuit of her photography degree, where Bryce, who is working towards his BSN, plans to move. I will heed your advice and *try* not to worry. I know in the end it will all work out exactly the way it's supposed to like it has a million times before. The only difference now is that you will be watching from above.

June 2019: It's been a little over a year. I have lived, survived, even thrived without my dad. I've had to make decisions, and I've had trying times. I still talk to my dad and ask him for guidance. "What would Dad say," I ask myself over and over. I talk out loud to him. I reminisce and say, "Remember when dad…?"

As I've read this memoir at least a dozen times, I've experienced many moments that made me cry. I mean sobbing, eyes red and puffy kind of crying. I've relived memories that made me smile or laugh out loud. It's hard for me to comprehend that a year, 365 days and nights, Christmas, birthdays, vacations, all of these have gone by and my dad is not a part of them.

I am a *huge* fan of the TV show, *The Golden Girls.* I have watched every episode at least 20 times! I can recite most of the scenes and still laugh at my favorite ones even though I know exactly what is coming and recall all the punchlines. There is one episode in particular that always gets to me. For those who are not familiar, Blanche's (Rue McClanahan) father dies. Blanche is the slutty Southern belle of the show who is also a daddy's girl. At first, she is in denial, unable to comprehend or believe that her father, the man who has been her rock, her hero, all of her life, is gone. After some convincing, Dorothy (Bea Arthur) convinces Blanche that she needs this time and closure and that going to Atlanta to attend her father's funeral would help her.

The last scene of this episode is where I always watch intently and cry. The funeral for her father is over. The scene takes place in a simple, Southern-style cemetery. Blanche is surrounded by headstones of various shapes and sizes, a large oak tree draped in Spanish moss, colorful flowers strewn about and the sounds of nature and birds in the background. Blanche is standing at her father's gravesite, talking to him, thanking him for everything, even bringing up moments when she was an unruly teenager. She asks her mom, who is buried next to him, to take care of him. Blanche is unaware that Dorothy is standing in the background until Dorothy quietly interrupts and tells Blanche that they need to leave for the airport if they are to make their flight. Blanche's face is somber, sad. She turns and walks towards Dorothy. She stops, turns, and takes a final look at her father's grave and says, "Dorothy, I'm nobody's little girl anymore."

Author Bio

Cynthia Beardslee was raised in the beautiful mountains of northwestern New Jersey. Although living in North Carolina for the past 27 years, she will always be a Jersey Girl at heart. After raising two children, she found herself an empty nester. With a longstanding desire to write, she jumped right in, and this memoir was born.

She intends to continue writing, with plans for living on her 36-foot sailboat, *MeandHer* with the love of her life, and to enjoy sailing along the eastern coast and the Bahamas.

Lightning Source UK Ltd.
Milton Keynes UK
UKHW010225161221
395721UK00001B/192